YES YOU CAN

ACE SCHOOL WITHOUT LOSING YOUR MIND

First published 2020 by Macmillan

This edition published 2022 by Macmillan
an imprint of Pan Macmillan
The Smithson, 6 Briset Street, London EC1M 5NR
EU representative: Macmillan Publishers Ireland Ltd, 1st Floor,
The Liffey Trust Centre, 117–126 Sheriff Street Upper
Dublin 1, D01 YC43
Associated companies throughout the world
www.panmacmillan.com

ISBN 978-1-0350-0532-1

Text copyright © Natasha Devon 2020 and 2022
Illustrations © Rubyetc 2020

The right of Natasha Devon and Rubyetc to be identified as the author and illustrator of this work has been asserted by them in accordance with the Copyright, Designs and Patents Act 1988.

All rights reserved. No part of this publication may be reproduced, stored in a retrieval system, or transmitted, in any form or by any means (electronic, mechanical, photocopying, recording or otherwise), without the prior written permission of the publisher.

Pan Macmillan does not have any control over, or any responsibility for, any author or third-party websites referred to in or on this book.

1 3 5 7 9 8 6 4 2

A CIP catalogue record for this book is available from the British Library.

Design: Perfect Bound Ltd

Printed and bound by CPI Group (UK) Ltd, Croydon CR0 4YY

This book is sold subject to the condition that it shall not, by way of trade or otherwise, be lent, resold, hired out, or otherwise circulated without the publisher's prior consent in any form of binding or cover other than that in which it is published and without a similar condition including this condition being imposed on the subsequent purchaser.

Picture Credits

Rubyetc: 3, 9, 10, 20, 21, 23, 31, 46, 63, 64, 76, 87, 92, 104-5, 153, 165, 193, 197. **istockphoto:** kjohansen 111. **Shutterstock:** Africa Studio 132, 136; aimy27feb 8; Alona_S 15; Anatolir 15t; ANNA ZASIMOVA 163; art nick 133; Atomazul 68bl; Bonezboyz 139; cobalt88 110; Dmitry Lobanov 50; Ecelop 61; Eric Isselee 82, 102; Featureflash Photo Agency 68tl; Frame Art 179; Hanna Lehun 81b; Hurst Photo 97; Indayani 58; Jacky Co 66; jakkapan 19; jaroslava V 26; Jolygon 16, 17, 29, 30, 200; Jstone 69tr; judyjump 92; Kathy Hutchins 69tl; Katrine Glazkova 96; Kindlena 88; Leremy 44, 45; LplusD 5; Marish 157; Natalia Toropova 164-165; Oguz Aral 91; optimarc 129, 188-191; Péter Gudella 120; Petr Toman 68tr; Richard Griffin 117-119; Robert Adrian Hillman 24; Rtimages 75, 125; S-F 100; Sashkin 193; Sudowoodo 15m & b, 83, 86, 87, 137; sumstudio49 19; Twocoms 68br; TZIDO SUN 138; volkova natalia 28, 34; voyata 110; whitelightgrapher 120; WildlifeWorld 81t. **Wikimedia Commons:** 71.

YES YOU CAN
ACE SCHOOL WITHOUT LOSING YOUR MIND

By Natasha Devon

Illustrated by Rubyetc

MACMILLAN

CONTENTS

INTRODUCTION	1
SECTION 1	
UNDERSTANDING YOUR BRAIN	14
SECTION 2	
STUDYING	40
SECTION 3	
PREPARATION AND TIME MANAGEMENT	90
SECTION 4	
TESTS AND EXAMS	126
SECTION 5	
THE NEXT CHAPTER	164
SECTION 6	
THE CONTRACT	190
CONCLUSION	195
FURTHER INFORMATION, ADVICE & SUPPORT	200

INTRODUCTION

ASK ANY TEENAGER to list the causes of anxiety, stress and general mental anguish in their life, the chances are **'academic anxiety'** will appear near the top. I know this because it's *literally* my job to ask teenagers to list causes of anxiety, stress and general mental anguish in their lives.

For more than a decade I've been visiting an average of three schools and colleges every week throughout the UK and beyond, delivering talks and conducting research on mental health, body image and gender equality. I work with 14-18-year-olds and use the information they give me to get a better understanding of what hinders, motivates and interests them. In turn, I use this information to create presentations and workshops (together with experts in psychology and neuroscience), as well as campaigning for changes which will better support the needs and interests of under-25s.

My job regularly takes me to Parliament, where I have terrific fun telling off politicians, and to TV studios, where I explain to commentators who think they're being terribly clever when they use terms like **'generation snowflake'** why they're definitely not. I like to think of myself as having created a platform for young people, many of whom cannot vote and are therefore more likely to have their needs and interests ignored.

To do my job, I have to listen - and I mean *really* listen and be prepared to have my assumptions challenged. It'd be far easier to be one of those people who says *'I remember what it was like to be a teenager'* and create my classes and campaigns on the basis of my recollections, but to do so would be to ignore two fundamental factors:

The first is that our brain has a tendency towards rose-tinted nostalgia. That's why adults often describe their teenage years as 'the best of their life' (they almost definitely weren't). They're cherry-picking the aspects of teenage life they wish they had now (no mortgage/taxes/wrinkles) and forgetting everything else (hormones/homework/heartbreak).

The second is that our frames of reference are radically different. It's absolutely true what my mum told me when I was about 13 – for example, that the things I was teased for at school (being swotty and having big lips) are some of the aspects of myself I appreciate most now, as an adult. Mum also predicted I would bump into the first person who broke my heart one day and think *'Eurgh. What did I ever see in them?'* Both of those premonitions came to pass, but hearing that wasn't the slightest comfort to me at the time. In fact, to my teenage ears it sounded a lot like my mum belittling my problems.

Similarly, when a family friend said to me – just days after I'd got the (excellent) A level results I had chucked every ounce of effort for the past two years into obtaining – *'after the first couple of days at uni, no one will ask or care what you got in your A levels'*. I felt the overwhelming urge to scream in his face forever (I didn't, you'll be relieved to learn).

When it comes to the role that assessments, exams and grades will play in your life, there's no point in my telling you what I know, with the benefit of hindsight. I can only work with what young people tell me they're going through, right now. And having had countless conversations with hundreds of teenagers, what I have gleaned is this:

> **YOU'D RATHER ACE EVERY BIT OF SCHOOLWORK AND LOSE YOUR MIND THAN NURTURE YOUR MENTAL WELLBEING AND GET A LOWER GRADE.**

THE MESSAGE I HAVE RECEIVED HAS BEEN LOUD AND UNEQUIVOCAL:

YOUNG PEOPLE ARE HYPER-AWARE THEIR MENTAL HEALTH IS IMPORTANT...

BUT, FOR A VARIETY OF REASONS, DOING WELL AT SCHOOL IS MORE IMPORTANT TO THEM.

WHETHER OR NOT I AGREE IS IMMATERIAL: THIS IS OUR STARTING POINT.

IS IT A BINARY CHOICE, THOUGH?

If, like the people I've described above, you're of the staunch opinion that grades are more important than your wellbeing, I'm **not** here to challenge that. I will, however, ask you **why you think you have to choose?**

Where has the idea that academic learning and mental health are at odds with one another come from? I suspect the answer is, in part, the media. TV and radio shows are forever pitting stereotypical **'trads'** (people who think education was better when pupils were seen and not heard, did their homework using a quill by candlelight and were thrashed with canes if they didn't hand it in on time) and **'progs'** (people who think schools should do away with reading altogether and pupils should instead go and sit under a tree to write a song about the beauty of a blade of grass, at the end of which everyone will get a medal for participating)* for entertainment value.

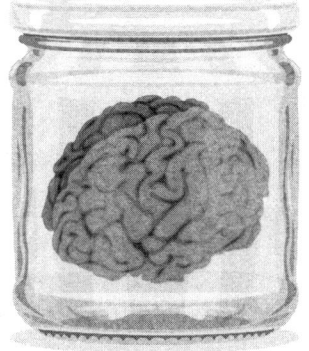

Similarly, schools often have 'wellbeing weeks', as though having a relationship with your body and mind is an endeavour you can choose to opt out of. It would be a great deal more convenient, I am sure, if we had the facility to open a door in our foreheads, scoop out our brains and plop them into a jar to sit in a classroom somewhere, absorbing everything we needed to know while we got on with the other aspects of life. Unfortunately, at the time of writing, this is a feat beyond the scope of human endeavour.

---

*   *These *might* be slightly reductive characterizations, FYI.*

Everything is connected. Your physical fitness affects your mental health and the wellbeing of your mind impacts your ability to learn. Perhaps most excitingly, academic learning has been shown in numerous studies to make us happier and healthier.

Furthermore, there is a **sweet spot**, consisting of activities proven to make you a more effective learner and which also, handily, improve your **mental fitness** (see page 9 to find out what I mean by this). Imagine it like a Venn diagram, with academic attainment on the left and mental health on the right.

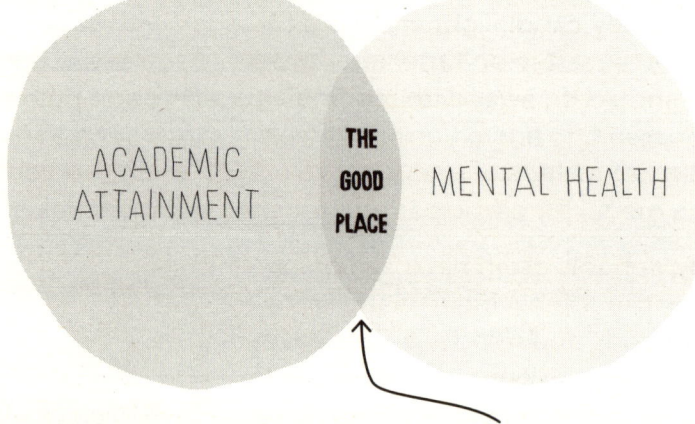

THIS BOOK is an exploration of the point at which the worlds of academia and wellbeing meet. Its aim is to make you more likely to achieve the highest grade of which you are capable, as well as emerging with your mental health and self-esteem intact – even improved. It's going to allow you to understand your brain better, as well as give you practical guidance and exercises to help you through your schooldays, and all the challenges, assessments and exams that these years bring.

Here are a few things to bear in mind, before we begin:

WHAT IS 'MENTAL HEALTH'?

Lots of people use the terms **'mental health'** and **'mental illness'** interchangeably. I often hear 'mental health is on the increase in the UK' or 'my sister had mental health, once'.

These statements don't make sense. To understand why, substitute the word 'mental' for 'physical' – in just the same way as everyone has an objective overall level of physical health, absolutely everyone has a level of mental health.

Similarly, the phrase **'mental health issues'** covers an incredibly broad remit. Anything that impacts the way you think, feel about yourself, relate to others and perceive the world in turn affects your mental health.

There is endless debate over how these various terms should be used and the conversation is constantly shifting.

However, when I say **mental health issue** I mean anything that originates in the mind and **negatively** impacts our ability to function.

When I say **mental illness** I mean a condition which would be recognized by a medical professional as meeting a set of criteria which would lead them to diagnose an illness.

Stress, for example, is (in my opinion) a mental health issue. However, it is **not** a diagnosable mental illness in the same way as clinical depression or bipolar disorder, unless it is very severe.

There is a lot of talk at the moment about the dangers of 'medicalizing normal emotions' when we discuss mental health. I think that's probably a reflection of how inadequate the term **mental health issue** is for discussing specific states of being. After all, if I told you I had a 'physical health issue' it would be absolutely ludicrous for me to expect you to understand exactly what I meant by that – my malady could be anything from a broken leg, to diabetes, to having accidentally wedged a Haribo strawberry in my left nostril (actually happened to a friend of mine).

Similarly, to acknowledge that sometimes young people get colds and need to drink lots of fluids and rest isn't 'medicalizing childhood'. When encountering everyday types of anxiety (distinct from anxiety disorders – see next chapter), stress or insecurity, we need the mental health equivalent of a cough sweet and a lie-down. By recognizing this we aren't making any kind of diagnosis (other than the very serious one of **'being human'**).

To help understand the kind of 'mental health' we are addressing in this book, look at the graph below:

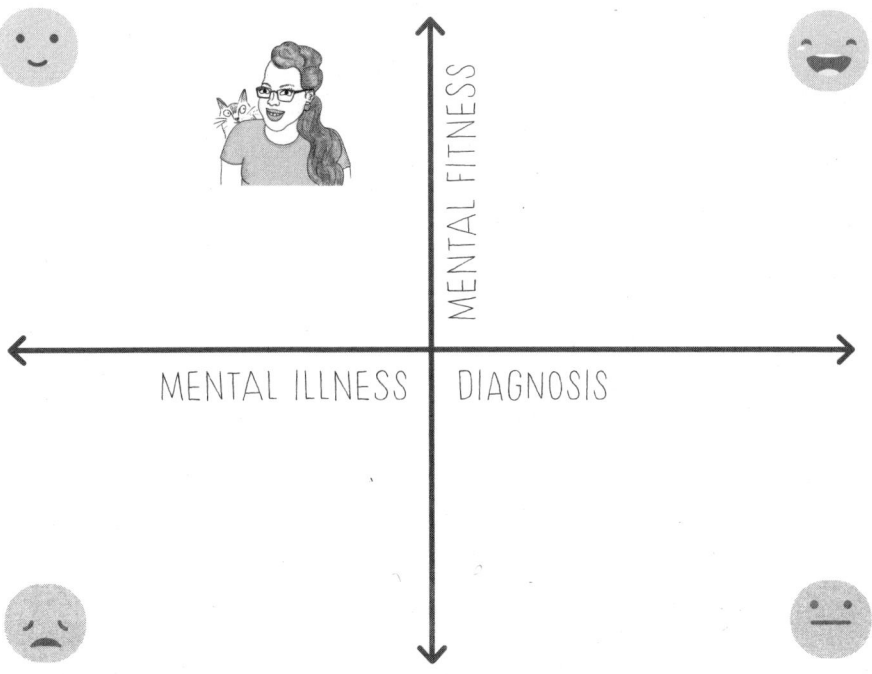

The horizontal axis represents **mental illness diagnosis.** Everyone exists at some point between the two binaries – with the furthest left being a person with a diagnosis of severe mental illness and the furthest right a person with no diagnosis at all.

The vertical axis is **mental fitness.** This is what is often referred to in schools as 'resilience' (although I don't particularly care for the term). It represents the strategies and tools a person has at their disposal to be able to deal with any challenges they might face.

Take a moment to consider where you are on this graph.

I, for example, am left of centre because I have a diagnosis of a moderate mental illness (Panic Disorder) but towards the top of the vertical access because my mental fitness is fairly high. That's a good place to be (hence Ruby has captured me in an expression of happiness). Your aim is to keep yourself in the top half of the graph.

(Do feel free to draw your own version, adding yourself at your current place on the spectrum).

Even if you have no diagnosis, it's still important to keep your mental fitness as **high** as possible. That's because our position on the spectrum isn't fixed – it changes in response to the circumstances and challenges we face. A person with no diagnosis of mental illness but with very poor mental fitness, for example, might develop depression and find themselves in the bottom left, which is the quarter of the spectrum we're trying to avoid. If you think you are in the bottom left of the graph now, please don't despair. As I've said already, our position in the spectrum is never, ever permanent. Improving your mental fitness can take you to the top left (welcome to my quadrant!) and, depending whether your mental health diagnosis is short or long term, eventually into the top right.

The activities in this book are designed to help you strengthen the vertical axis, an endeavour which is relevant and important no matter who you are.

YOUR BRAIN IS UNIQUE

You should approach each of the activities in this book on the basis that they **might** work. Embrace them with enthusiasm, give them a chance, but if they aren't helping, you shouldn't hesitate in ditching them.

There are any number of factors – neurological, psychological and environmental – that can affect the way you absorb information and learn. For example, I absolutely cannot bear to have any sort of music playing whilst I'm writing, yet writer-friends of mine claim to be at their most productive against a backdrop of 'white noise' created by soft classical tunes, whilst others like to crank up death metal to ear-bleeding levels.

I actually find I remember a presentation less if the presenter has a text-dense powerpoint and proceeds to read it word for word to the audience (in fact, this style makes my soul wither, which is why if I've ever been to your school you'll have noticed I only use pictures in my slides). It's like my eyes say to my ears 'assuming you've got this, I'm going to have a rest' and vice versa. A friend of mine with dyslexia, however, is able to recall information better if she hears and sees it simultaneously.

Throughout this book, you'll find **quizzes** which will help you to determine what kind of learner you are and tailored **techniques** for you to try to find the best way for you to learn. If something works for a friend but not for you it's not a reflection of your respective abilities, just that they have a brain that works in a different way to yours.

WHAT QUALIFIES ME TO WRITE ABOUT SCHOOL?

Over the years I've done extensive research into adolescent mental health, but what (I hear you cry) qualifies me to write about grades and learning?

Well, don't hate me, but I've aced every exam I've ever done (apart from one which I will talk about later). In fact, I actually enjoy them. I loved almost every aspect of school (I appreciate I am beginning to sound weird now).

At university, because of a perfect storm of circumstances I have since referred to as an 'omnishambles' (a couple of traumatic events, my anxiety becoming turbo-charged and blossoming into an eating disorder, and using alcohol as a coping mechanism) my academic life became fairly non-existent. I'm not exaggerating when I say I can count on my fingers and toes the number of lectures and seminars I attended during the entirety of my degree.

I've since discovered that learning and mental health have what is called a 'symbiotic' relationship i.e. they influence one another. When we're really engaged in and passionate about what we're learning, that gives a sense of purpose and achievement, both of which are key human psychological needs. If what we're doing at school is creative, it also releases endorphins (more on these later) which are essential to mental health. So, whilst I wasn't able to learn at university because my mental health had deteriorated so much, it's also true to say that the not learning would have contributed to my poor state of wellbeing, at the time.

> **'I DON'T THINK DOING WELL IN SCHOOL IS ALWAYS THE SAME THING AS BEING CLEVER.'**

Having said that, I don't think doing well in school is always the same thing as being clever. Most subjects are mainly assessed by our exam grades, in the end. The ability to ace a test under timed conditions mostly requires the combination of two particular skills – the first is the ability to remain calm in the face of pressure and the second is a good memory. Both of these are learnable and both are skills that can be strengthened with the techniques in this book. One day, perhaps we'll have a fundamental revolution in the education system whereby exams are finally acknowledged as an inadequate tool for measuring intelligence. Until that time, however, they are something that the vast majority of humankind have to endure.

And on that note, let us begin . . .

SECTION 1
UNDERSTANDING YOUR BRAIN

YOUR BRAIN – AN OVERVIEW

THE AVERAGE ADULT BRAIN is heavier than you'd expect, at 1.5 kilograms. That's the same as **480 teabags...**

75 pieces of sushi . . .

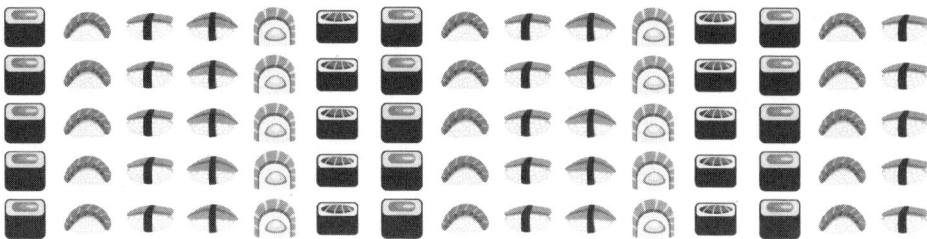

15 blueberry muffins . . .

10 medium-sized bananas . . .

. . . or **one and a half pineapples**. Little wonder, then, that studies show around 10% of the population is suffering from neck pain at any given time – that's a lot of brain to carry around all day.

THE BRAIN IS DIVIDED INTO TWO HEMISPHERES – LEFT AND RIGHT.

You've probably heard people who are good at maths or coding described as **'left-brained'** ...

... whilst musicians and artists have a reputation for being **'right-brained'**.

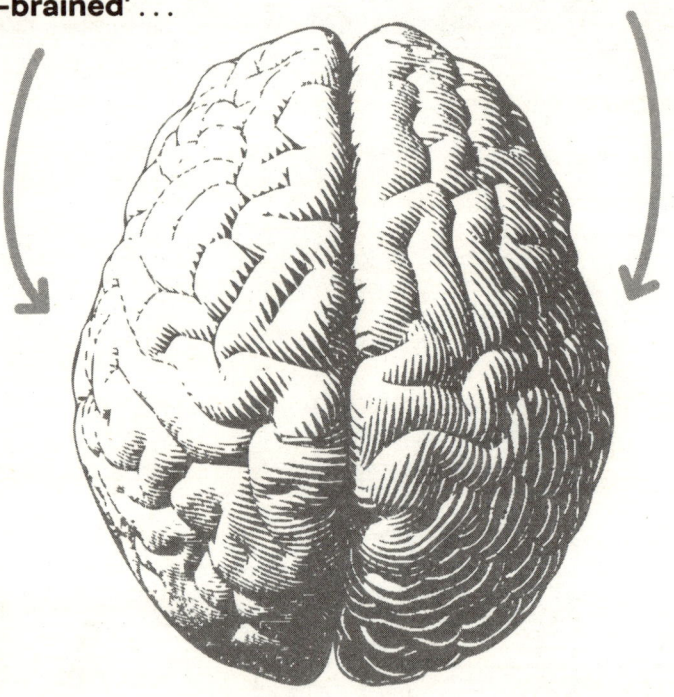

This is based on a misunderstanding about how the brain actually works. Whilst it is true that each half of the brain is responsible for different skills – the left more analytical and the right more creative – it's a **total myth** that people are either 'left- or right-brained'. In fact, almost everything you do involves **both sides** of your brain working together to some extent.

AS WELL AS LEFT AND RIGHT, THE BRAIN IS DIVIDED INTO FOUR LOBES.

Your **occipital lobe** is right at the back of your skull and its main function is to process visual information received from your eyes.

In the middle section, your **parietal lobe** is at the top. This processes sensory information such as touch and sound, which is why it's very important for language. It is also responsible for navigation and recognition of pain.

Your **temporal lobe** interprets sensory input and draws meanings from them, in turn creating an emotional narrative which helps you make sense of the world.

Your brain develops back to front, so the last part to 'come online' is your **frontal lobe**, situated just behind your forehead. It is responsible for subtle and complicated aspects of human behaviour, such as problem solving, judgement, impulse control and how we relate to each other on a social level.

YOUR PARIETAL, TEMPORAL AND FRONTAL LOBES ALL CONTAIN ELEMENTS OF WHAT IS KNOWN AS THE

'LIMBIC SYSTEM'.

THIS IS SOMETIMES REFERRED TO AS THE

'EMOTIONAL BRAIN'

AND IT PLAYS A KEY ROLE NOT JUST IN MENTAL HEALTH, AS YOU MIGHT EXPECT, BUT ALSO IN THE LEARNING PROCESS . . .

One of the first parts of your limbic system to develop is the **amygdala**. The amygdala has one seemingly simple but fundamental job – to keep you alive. It is not concerned with context – it has no sense of the past or future and it doesn't have any morality. As such, it is constantly scanning the area around you for evidence of a threat to your existence, or the opportunity for instant reward. If it perceives a threat it will initiate a strong and immediate response – dispatching chemicals to the rest of the body using your brain's (vastly more efficient) version of DHL, known as **neurotransmitters**.

I like to think of the amygdala as a cross between a siren and an automatic soap dispenser (because I'm odd that way). When danger is detected, your amygdala alerts the rest of the brain and body, causing it to prepare us for **fight, flight or freeze** (see page 33) by changing our chemical balance.

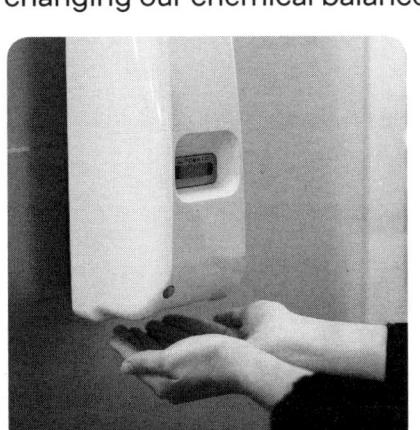

This would be fine, except the amygdala is a fairly unsophisticated radar and its idea of what constitutes a threat to life can be, to put it mildly, rather daft. We will come to this later in the section on anxiety.

Fortunately, at around eight months old, we develop two **septal nuclei** – one for each hemisphere of the brain. These have the ability to inhibit the amygdala, so we aren't just running around punching things all day. Have you ever seen those reins people attach to toddlers so they can walk within a limited radius of their care-giver and have a certain amount of freedom within safe parameters? The septal nuclei are the reins to your amygdala's over-excitable infant.

There are other brain parts involved in the limbic system which I won't detail here (including the **hippocampi**, which look like seahorses and are therefore quite fun), but it's important to understand how it affects learning and wellbeing simultaneously.

The limbic system is responsible for secreting the vast majority (93%) of your total levels of a chemical called **dopamine**.

Dopamine's job is to excite your brain cells, which makes it crucial for motivation, learning and concentration.

You've probably heard dopamine spoken about in relation to all kinds of addictions, from drugs to smart-phones. Whilst it's true that anything addictive increases the amount of dopamine in our brains in a way that can cause us to become dysfunctional, the chemical also plays an important role in brain health. It's getting the right balance which is key. **Too much** dopamine causes hyperactivity, whereas **too little** can lead to diseases of the nervous system (such as Parkinson's).

We can see, then, that even on a chemical level your ability to learn is inextricably linked with your mental wellbeing.

The really interesting thing about dopamine is that during your teenage years most people will experience a natural (and completely normal) spike. Which brings me to . . .

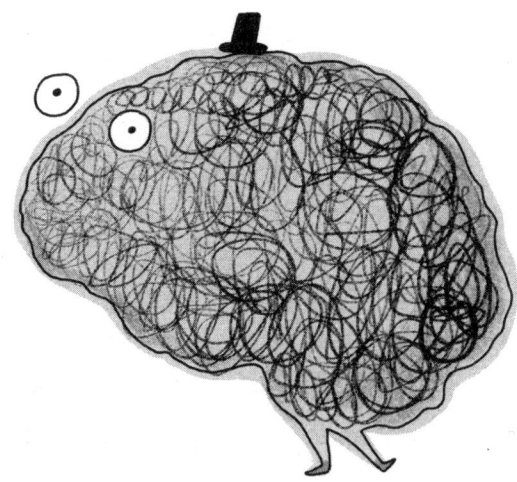

THE TEENAGE BRAIN

Society deems we become adults at **18**. I don't know who decided that, but whoever it was didn't know much about the human brain. Our brains don't actually finish developing until we are around **24 years old**.

That doesn't mean, however, that we are children until then. In fact, the adolescent brain is completely unique and, in my humble opinion, totally **brilliant**. The bulk of my work is with teenagers and I love the way they're smart enough to understand how the world works but open-minded enough to want it to change. Teenagers also think completely 'outside of the box'. If 'the box' was in, say, Paris, a teenager's ideas generally come from somewhere near Pluto. This prevents my job from ever being boring.

As it turns out, there are very good reasons why teenagers are like this. Dr David Bainbridge, who is a Reproductive Biologist at Cambridge University specializing in adolescence, told me that our teenage years are when the 'complex tangle of connections between brain cells which are developed during childhood are trimmed and neatened to produce the efficient thinking machine which makes humans so special'. In fact, your brain is larger at 10 years of age than it is at 20.

Yet (in theory at least) a 20-year-old is **smarter** than a 10-year-old, so this pruning phase is meant to make our brain's functioning more streamlined. Teenagers therefore have the combined curiosity of a child with some of the advanced cognitive skills that adults have.

Adolescence is also the time when we get our 'third layer' of awareness, which means that instead of focusing solely on our immediate surroundings, we are easily distracted. (Anyone who has ever tried to present to a class of teenagers and suddenly heard 'SNOOOOOOOOW' or 'BEEEEEEEEEEE!' will attest to this.)

Having said all of this, you cannot alter the fact that you are a teenager. It's advantageous to know what stage of development your brain is at and that many of the ways you are thinking and behaving will feel unfamiliar. But it's not like you can do much about the fact that, for example, your brain is secreting unprecedented levels of dopamine during adolescence, making you more prone to **risk-taking behaviour**.

Instead, it's more helpful to focus on the ways your brain is **better equipped for studying** than it has ever been before. Dr Bainbridge points to your new organizational abilities. 'Unlike children,' he says, 'teenagers can respond to finding a task easy or difficult by organizing their work, prioritizing what's important and focusing on their goals'.

You'll find out how to harness these new abilities in Section 2.

'In some ways, it's strange that adolescence is when we are asked to sit exams,' says Dr Bainbridge. 'Between 16 and 18 you're really just learning to use your new-found cognitive brilliance'. Part of the reason the process feels so hard is because you're still getting used to your new brain skills. If exams happened in your early 30s, for example, you'd be used to practising self-analysis, which allows you to learn from mistakes and track where you have gone wrong.

WHY DON'T I PERFORM TO MY BEST ABILITY DURING AN EXAM?

EXAMS ARE A **STRANGE** AND **UNIQUE** PHENOMENON, WHEN YOU THINK ABOUT IT.

WHEN ELSE IN LIFE DO YOU HAVE ALL YOUR PERSONAL POSSESSIONS TAKEN AWAY FROM YOU AND GET HERDED, SINGLE FILE AND IN SILENCE, TO SIT AT A SMALL TABLE TO RECALL A HUGE NUMBER OF FAIRLY ARBITRARY FACTS, UNDER TIMED CONDITIONS, WITHOUT RECOURSE TO GOOGLE?

NEVER, THAT'S WHEN.

It would be odd, therefore, if you didn't feel at least a little bit apprehensive, both at the prospect of and during your exams. Indeed, most of the people I know who are in their thirties, forties and beyond still have the occasional exam-themed anxiety dream in the run-up to a stressful life event (mostly they're back sitting an exam for their least favourite subject and have the sudden realization that **a)** they haven't done any revision and **b)** they're naked). Exams have become a symbol within their subconscious of 'something I am dreading'.

?

Assessments and exams are also a human invention. They don't exist in nature – one doesn't see a teenage giraffe having to write a paper detailing the specific significant dates in the history of giraffe-dom before it's allowed to join the herd.

The human brain and body evolved during radically different times, when we lived a tribal existence that was more similar to that of other animals. Danger, in the context of tribal life, meant the prospect of being attacked by a predator or some other life-threatening event. Our physical responses to 'danger' signals from our brains (i.e. the chemical changes which create feelings of stress and anxiety) are therefore dramatic because, for a tribesperson, the situation usually was.

We have all the same basic hardware that a caveperson had, but we are living in a radically different society. Stress and anxiety are therefore best described as ancient reactions which often aren't appropriate for modern life. It is for that reason that so many of us hand in our homework, or walk out of class feeling like we haven't performed to the best of our ability. Intellectual pursuits are best undertaken when we are relaxed. In situations when we are stressed or anxious, our minds and bodies go into autopilot and don't seem to obey our commands, however much we prepare.

How do you get round this? The first step is to understand what is happening in the mind and body in response to stress and anxiety.

STRESS

Which of the following best sums up your reaction to being stressed:

> 'The greatest weapon against stress is our ability to choose one thought over another.'
> **William James**
> American Philosopher
> (1842-1910)

1 I push through it and carry on: stress is for weaklings!

2 I talk to my friends and we try to come up with reasons why I'm feeling the way I do.

3 I work harder and longer and hope the stress will eventually go away.

If number 1 is most like you, you could be in **denial** about stress. If you're number 2, chances are you're **stressing** about stress. People who choose number 3 usually **overwork** themselves and inadvertently create more stress. All of these can lead to becoming caught up in a counterproductive stress cycle.

Our reactions to stress are usually **learned behaviours** and based on fundamental misunderstandings about what stress is and the role it performs in our lives. Most people I speak to think of stress as something to be either feared or denied. They tell me they 'never feel stressed' with a proud, defiant lift of their chin as though this marks them out for future greatness. Or they confess in a hushed whisper that they often fall prey to feelings of stress, as though I'm going to immediately diagnose them with some terrible, rare affliction.

Stress, like so many of the topics we'll discuss in this book, has fallen victim to the modern tendency towards binary thinking. In reality, it can be either a positive or negative influence in our lives, depending on context and extent.

STRESS IS USEFUL

We humans lean towards **laziness**. I imagine this has something to do with early people conserving calories for hunting and gathering, rather than wasting energy on fruitless ambling about. Whenever you feel that irresistible urge to take to your bed for a day and devour an entire season on Netflix whilst WhatsApping your siblings with increasingly imaginative methods of bribery/favour-promising in return for them bringing you sustenance, that's actually your ancient biology in action.

Without stress, humans would **do nothing** but lie around like walruses.

We also wouldn't have survived this long. In evolutionary terms, those humans who felt the sensation of stress would have been more likely to get off their behinds, in turn meaning they were less likely to be found and mauled to death by predators.
The physical feelings we associate with stress therefore had to be unpleasant, to motivate us towards action.

Our stress hormones are **cortisol** and the less infamous (and less catchy) **DHEA**. In small, short-term doses, these hormones improve our performance and brain capacity by sending energy in the form of glucose around our bodies and focusing our attention on what needs to be done.

TOO MUCH STRESS STOPS US LEARNING

Life is, however, more consistently stressful than the human body has evolved for. The modern world is a fraught and frantic place – full of noises, sights and situations not found in nature.

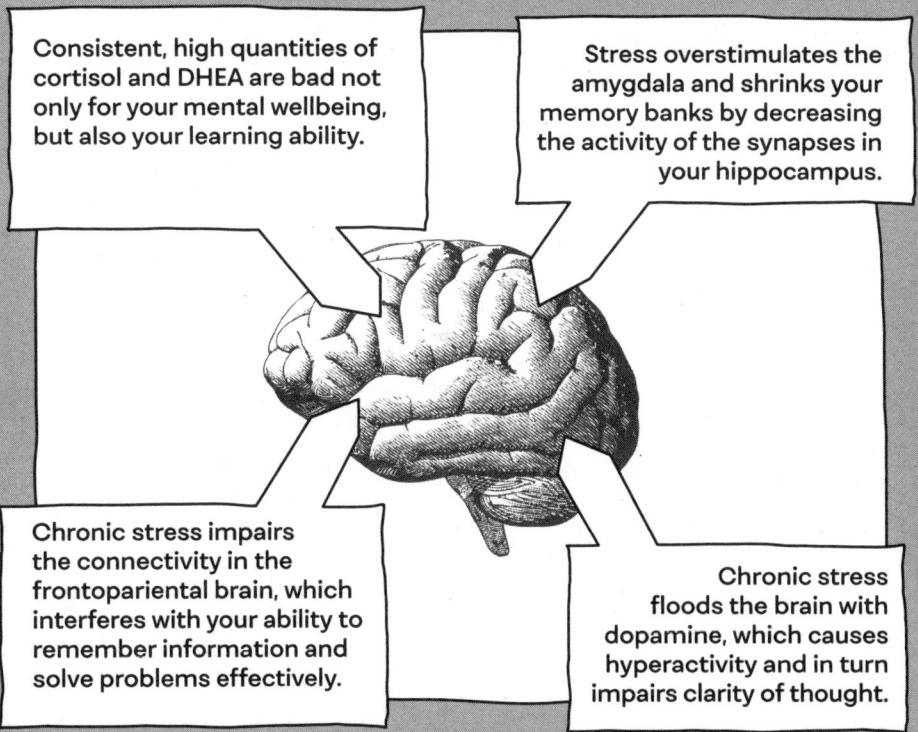

Consistent, high quantities of cortisol and DHEA are bad not only for your mental wellbeing, but also your learning ability.

Stress overstimulates the amygdala and shrinks your memory banks by decreasing the activity of the synapses in your hippocampus.

Chronic stress impairs the connectivity in the frontoparietal brain, which interferes with your ability to remember information and solve problems effectively.

Chronic stress floods the brain with dopamine, which causes hyperactivity and in turn impairs clarity of thought.

Highly stressed people therefore have impaired judgement, cloudy thoughts and a heightened sense that something terrible is about to happen. This is very far from an ideal state to be in when you're trying to stay in a mindset that opens you up to learning.

THE 'RIGHT AMOUNT' OF STRESS

Stress is a bit like caffeine – a small amount directly before an important event might make you feel more alert, but if you're habitually necking eight giant energy drinks a day the chances are you're not functioning particularly well. The key is to identify the 'right' amount – that which will focus your attention without curtailing your ability to problem solve.

The ability to control stress is a subtle art, but it basically comes down to two skills:

1. TRY NOT TO STRESS ABOUT STRESS.

We all do this to an extent, partly because stress is an uncomfortable feeling and our instinct is often to try to imagine a 'reason' to match the sensation. Our brains are, however, locked away in the darkness of our skulls. They're just a piece of **electrified blancmange** with no ability to distinguish between real and imagined causes of stress. For this reason, worry and conjecture will stimulate cortisol production, making us more stressed.

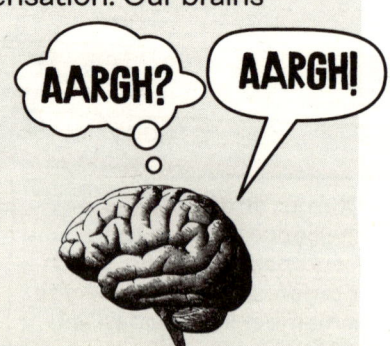

Instead of coming up with elaborate theories to justify stress, instead perceive it as your body giving you a well-intentioned kick up the bum.

Later in this book you'll find **mindfulness techniques** which will draw you into (and therefore help you to objectively assess) the moment you're in. The ability to separate those aspects of a situation which are within your control from those outside of it will help to stop you worrying yourself into a perpetual and debilitating stress cycle.

2. TAKE REGULAR REST AND RELAXATION.

We often try to compensate for stress by working harder and longer, which can in turn amplify cortisol production. There is a difference between listening to stress cues and using them to motivate you to meet that homework deadline or do a chunk of studying/hitting the books, for example, and taking this to the extreme and ditching all other activity in favour of revision, holing ourselves up in a fort made of blankets and avoiding daylight for weeks on end, like a vampire or other mythical creature.

As we will discover in the section on perfectionism (page 37), **more work does not automatically equal a better result** (if this seems counterintuitive to you please feel free to write it on a post-it note backwards and stick it to your forehead). There is a tipping point with stress – a stage at which it becomes unhelpful. In that spirit, we should seek to regularly empty our **'stress bucket'** (there is a section on this later) to keep our overall levels of stress both manageable and conducive to learning.

> 'Worrying is carrying tomorrow's load with today's strength – carrying two days at once. It is moving into tomorrow ahead of time. Worrying doesn't empty tomorrow of its sorrow, it empties today of its strength.'
> Corrie ten Boom
> Dutch watchmaker (1892-1983)

ANXIETY
THE AMBIGUITY OF ANXIETY

Like stress, anxiety has served humankind extremely well during the evolution process. Anxiety is our physical and emotional response to our amygdala's danger signals (see page 19).

As we know, the amygdala is a hugely efficient but not particularly sophisticated piece of neurological equipment. Its sole job is to alert us to the possibility of either imminent threat or instant gratification and it doesn't change or amend its behaviour in response to getting that wrong, or making us look like an idiot.

When our amygdala senses threat, it kick-starts an automatic bodily response – three primal reactions to help us survive encounters with danger:

> **FIGHT – HIT IT;**
>
> **FLIGHT – RUN AWAY FROM IT;**
>
> **FREEZE – REMAIN COMPLETELY STILL AND HOPE IT DOESN'T NOTICE US.**

FFF (as I shall call it henceforth) floods our body with a chemical called **adrenaline**, causing us to become temporarily super-charged. Adrenaline increases oxygen supply around the body, pumping our muscles so we are faster and stronger than we were just seconds before. (That's why there have been recorded incidents of parents whose children are about to be crushed by a car suddenly finding the strength and speed to intervene and lift the bonnet, when just a few days before they were struggling to unscrew a jar of marmalade.)

Adrenaline also makes us **sharper**, in a very specific way. Sounds become louder, colours more vivid. We are on hyper alert, ready to detect the smallest changes in our environment and to make split-second, instinctual choices.

This is all **fantastic** if the threat in question is an angry bear. It's a less useful response if what's making us anxious is schoolwork. After all, you can't punch the teacher and run away . . . That kind of behaviour is frowned upon. Unfortunately, our amygdala doesn't know the difference between a nearby snarling tigress and having to write an 800-word essay on the Third Reich by 8am the next day. It just knows the situation we're in isn't pleasant and it doesn't like it.

However, unlike a small smattering of stress, anxiety **isn't** going to improve your ability to perform under pressure. One of the mechanisms of the FFF response is to shut down the conscious mind – the part with which we have internal conversations. That's the part which might cause us to dither and hesitate in an unhelpful fashion during a life-threatening situation, but it's also crucial for fully engaging, intellectually.

Have you ever found yourself in any of the following states when you are feeling up against it?:

1. Drenched in sweat
2. Desperate for a wee, even though you went to the loo just moments ago
3. Feeling sick
4. Shaking
5. Seemingly unable to control your limbs
6. Itchy

All of these are symptoms of adrenaline and mean you were in FFF mode. What most people don't know, however, is that they're probably predisposed to one of these responses more than the others.

> **Which of these** most applies to you when you're stressed about homework, or struggling to concentrate in class?:
>
> **1** I have a tendency not to listen to or read the instructions or questions properly and therefore waste my time writing or doing something irrelevant.
>
> **2** Instead of focusing on my work, I spend time thinking of reasons I might be able to get out of it (like 'what if I was sick right now, or fainted?').
>
> **3** My mind goes completely blank and I find myself unable to recall anything I have learned.

If number 1 sounds most like you, you're a 'fight' responder, if you're more like number 2, you're a 'flight' person, and number 3 is a 'freeze' reaction. In Section 3 of this book, we discuss the best ways to get yourself out of FFF.

> **Interesting fact:** US psychologist Curtis Reisinger believes we have three more potential responses to danger: **Flooding** (suddenly feeling incredibly emotional), **Fawning** (submitting to the threat) and **Sleeping** (using sleep as an avoidance tactic to get out of a crisis situation).

HOW WOULD I KNOW IF I HAD AN ANXIETY DISORDER?

I'm often asked how you know when anxiety has spilled over from 'normal' to 'disorder'. The short answer to that question is: you wouldn't. The symptoms of mental illness are complex and difficult to see in yourself and it's incredibly important not to self-diagnose.

If, however, you find that you feel anxious all the time, or in response to situations others find pleasurable (like a party) to the extent that it stops you functioning, **book an appointment** with your school counsellor or doctor. They'll be able to get you a proper assessment.

If it turns out you do have an anxiety disorder, please know that they are manageable and it's possible to live with them successfully and happily. I know this because I have a diagnosis of Panic Disorder. It took a while to find the right combination of medication, therapeutic support and lifestyle changes to support my recovery, but now I can honestly say it's just a part of who I am, in the same way as if I had diabetes.

If you want more information and advice, there are some helpful organizations and resources listed at the back of this book.

PERFECTIONISM

The word **'perfectionist'** has become synonymous with a person who gives their absolute best to every task and therefore produces work of the highest standard. This isn't, however, how perfectionism works in reality.

How many of these statements apply to you?

- I never think anything I do is good enough
- I rarely feel proud of myself
- I beat myself up if I don't get the top grade
- I don't think I'm as intelligent as my friends, so I work harder to compensate
- If I don't think I'll be good at something, I'd rather not try
- I make excuses to avoid activities which fall outside my talents
- I have very high standards for myself
- Other people's opinions of me are very important to how I feel about myself
- I feel my friends and family have expectations of me that are too high
- I often go above and beyond the work set by my teacher
- I rarely feel satisfied with my accomplishments

If five or more apply to you, the chances are you are a perfectionist. You're probably praised a lot by your parents or teachers because you don't conform to the stereotype of the 'lazy teenager' but, from both a psychological and an academic perspective, the impact of perfectionism can be devastating. There are two main ways in which perfectionism can interfere with both your ability to learn and your mental health:

PERFECTIONISTS ARE NEVER SATISFIED AND THEREFORE WORK PAST THEIR 'PEAK' POINT.

The following graph was donated to this book by Dr Alan Barnard, who is the world's leading 'Decision Scientist' (I didn't know what this meant until I went to one of his lectures – basically, he's an expert on how to keep your brain sharp):

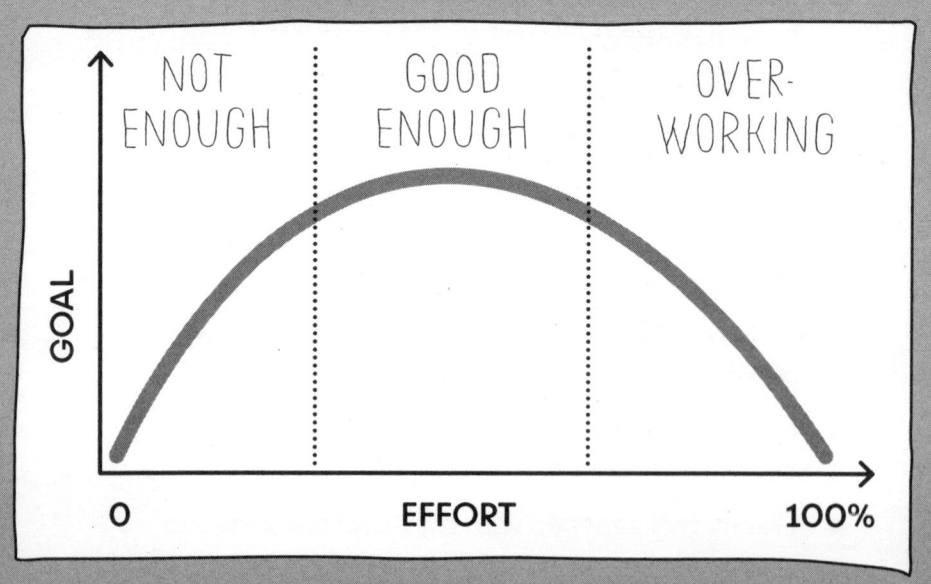

Graph: Y-axis labeled GOAL, X-axis labeled EFFORT from 0 to 100%. An inverted U-curve divided into three regions: NOT ENOUGH, GOOD ENOUGH, OVER-WORKING.

As you can see from the graph, perfection doesn't actually exist, there is only 'good enough'. If you regularly work past your 'peak point' in pursuit of perfection it becomes completely counterproductive. This is called 'the point of diminishing returns'. Overworking and associated stress actually impairs your cognitive ability, leaving you less able to recall information, solve problems and think creatively – all of which are absolutely key for learning, understanding and also for revision and exam performance.

PERFECTIONISTS AVOID ACTIVITIES OR SUBJECTS THEY DON'T THINK THEY'LL BE 'BEST' AT. THEY THEREFORE OFTEN DON'T ACHIEVE THE RESULTS THEY ARE CAPABLE OF IN SOME SUBJECTS BECAUSE THEY ARE AVOIDING ENGAGING WITH THEM AND TRYING THEIR BEST.

So, how do you ensure you don't work past the point of diminishing returns and keep your brain at its most efficient? Keep reading to find out...

SECTION 2
STUDYING

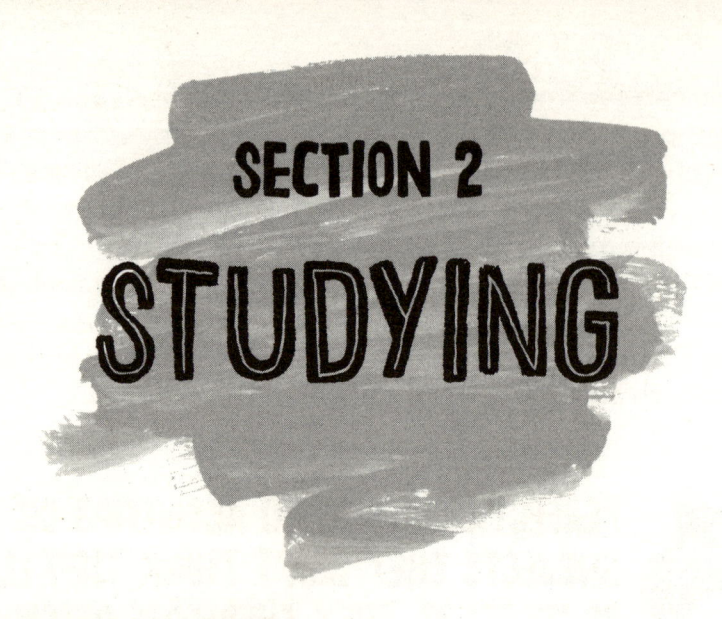

PROMISE CARD

When I first began writing this book, my intention was to explore where academic attainment and mental wellbeing overlapped. Yet, the more I researched the more I realized that it's pretty much **impossible** to have one without the other. I hope, in Section 1, I have managed to persuade you of this.

Yet I also know how easy it is to **forget this**, in a society that fetishizes playing Russian Roulette with your brain health in pursuit of superficial 'success'. To remind you, write a **promise** to yourself on a small piece of card.

It's best to put it in your own words, but you might choose something like:

> 'I WILL REMEMBER THAT STRESS DECREASES COGNITIVE ABILITY AND I SHOULD TAKE REGULAR BREAKS FROM STUDYING'

> 'I WILL PRIORITIZE SELF-CARE AS MUCH AS STUDY'

Or even just

> 'WORKING TOO HARD IS COUNTERPRODUCTIVE'

Keep it on you – in a pocket, wallet or notebook, to look at any time you feel your resolve wobble.

WORK-LIFE BALANCE

> 'Don't let the perfect be the enemy of the good.'
> *Italian proverb*

Dr Thomas Curran is one of the world's leading researchers on perfectionism. He has also done a brilliant TED Talk (see page 203 for the link) which I insist you watch **this instant.**

Seriously, put the book down and go and look it up.

Done? **Good.**

In Section 1 we looked at how stress and overwork can have a counterproductive impact, stopping us from learning and understanding and retaining information. I asked Dr Curran how you would know when you'd reached your 'point of diminishing returns', i.e. when working harder would actually impede studying.

He said that the easiest way to know you're working too hard is when studying has started to eat into the things that keep you healthy – both physically and mentally. Slowly, we tend to sacrifice our hobbies, time with friends and even habits we know are essential, like eating healthily, exercising and washing, since we often consider them **'less important'** than studying.

Yet, to do this is a **miscalculation** – since having a healthily functioning brain is arguably more important when you are studying and trying to retain information than it has ever been.

BEARING ALL THIS IN MIND, I'D LIKE YOU TO ATTEMPT SOMETHING TRULY RADICAL –

I WANT YOU TO PLAN YOUR STUDY AROUND YOUR LIFE, RATHER THAN THE OTHER WAY AROUND

(WHICH IS THE WAY MOST PEOPLE DO IT).

First of all, make a list of the things that keep you healthy and sane. Ideally, these would fall into four categories:

PHYSICAL ACTIVITY
(e.g. team sport, walking or running, yoga, gym, dancing around pretending to be Bruno Mars)

RELAXATION
(e.g. listening to music, playing video games, mindfulness or meditation)

SOCIALIZING
(e.g. being a member of a club or society such as the Guides, spending time with siblings or friends)

CREATIVITY
(e.g. writing in a journal, dance, drama, painting or drawing, coding, baking or crafts)

Some activities might belong in more than one category, e.g. dance is both physical activity and creative (if you do it as part of a club it can also be social).

FOR OPTIMUM MENTAL HEALTH, YOU WANT TO INCORPORATE ONE OF THE ACTIVITIES ABOVE FOR HALF AN HOUR EACH DAY AND ENGAGE IN AT LEAST 3 OF THE 4 CATEGORIES EVERY WEEK.

AIM FOR THREE SESSIONS OF PHYSICAL ACTIVITY IF POSSIBLE.

For example... Let's say you're in a football team, love gaming and have a pet dog called Geoff. Your basic mental health maintenance routine might look something like this:

HEY GEOFF, LESS POSING MORE POOTLING!

MON	TUES	WEDS	THUR	FRI	SAT	SUN
FOOTBALL PRACTICE	WALK GEOFF ROUND THE PARK	PRACTISE MINDFULNESS USING APP	WALK GEOFF ROUND THE PARK	GAME NIGHT WITH MATES	GAME NIGHT WITH MATES	PRACTISE MINDFULNESS USING APP

These are your fixtures and your study time should be planned around these activities.

The next thing to do is prioritize your study. Get three pieces of paper and head them:

SUBJECTS I ENJOY

SUBJECTS I DREAD

SUBJECTS I'M BEHIND ON

Try to be as **specific** as possible – for example, you might love and be up to date on learning about the Tudors for history, but have a mental block about the module on the Cold War.

Now it's time to work out which way of tackling these is most likely to motivate you. For each set of three statements below, work out which most applies to you:

STATEMENT 1

A I can take a while to get motivated to work, but once the juices are flowing I find it easy to get stuck in.

B I find it easier to do something I'm dreading if I can 'reward' myself afterwards.

C I can put off getting started on a project forever and often don't give myself enough time to do it properly.

STATEMENT 2

A Having an impending deadline motivates me to work – some of my best essays have been pulled out of the bag at the eleventh hour.

B Deadlines don't really mean that much to me, I'd rather get everything I have to do done as soon as possible and then be free to live my life.

C Having an impending deadline panics me to the extent I can't think straight and waste lots of time stressing.

STATEMENT 3

A I find I get more energy and enthusiasm to study as I go along.

B My favourite bit of studying is when it is OVER.

C Sometimes, I spend so long planning my study I don't have time to actually do it.

STATEMENT 4

A I stop studying when the section I've set myself is done, no matter how long that takes.

B I stop studying when I get bored.

C I stop studying when I'm so tired I fall asleep.

Mostly As

You're generally quite self-motivated and tend to enjoy studying just for the joy of knowing stuff. It's probably a good idea for you to start with a subject you enjoy to get yourself into a work headspace, but make sure you limit the time you spend on that and incorporate a subject you're dreading, or behind on, in each session.

You're also at the highest risk of burnout from overworking, so take extra care to schedule in the activities which keep you well, from the lists you've made above. Try also giving yourself one study-free day per week.

Mostly Bs

Your motto is 'but how is this relevant to my life, though?'. Whilst you're probably very bright, you often can't see the point of studying and would much rather learn by being out in the 'real' world, living.

You probably have quite a short attention span and are therefore in danger of letting your schoolwork slide. The key for you will be discovering your 'driving force' (see page 60) and giving yourself rewards after each session of study. Make sure you start with a subject you dislike, or are behind on, then progress to the topics you love later in your study session.

Mostly Cs

You are an epic procrastinator! See the next section to find out more about why we procrastinate.

Your biggest challenge is getting over your fear of failure and realizing you don't have to do everything at once. Adopt the motto 'any action is progress' and the old Italian proverb 'don't let the perfect be the enemy of the good'. Challenge yourself to just do one paragraph. You'll probably find by the time you get to the end, you'll want to do more.*

Hardly anything is as terrible in real life as it is in our imaginations, so try a subject you hate first. Remember, it's just one paragraph.

---

* Whilst I was definitely a category A person at school, I adopted this technique with exercise (which I often find difficult to motivate myself to do). I'd say I was just going to go to the gym and do 15 minutes on the cross trainer, but by the time I'd done that I was usually in the mood for a full workout.

WHY DO I PROCRASTINATE?

It's generally a myth that people who procrastinate are **'lazy'**. In fact, if you could see inside their head, you'd find a lot of activity – worrying about outcomes, anxieties about not being good enough and fretting about where to start on their giant to-do lists.

Procrastination can often be a **perfectionist** trait, born out of not wanting to get anything wrong (if you never start then technically you can't fail).

A fear of failure is actually something our society teaches us. We aren't born with it – you don't see toddlers trying to walk, falling over and declaring they 'just can't do it' before sitting on their nappy-clad bums for evermore.

If you are procrastinating, take a few minutes to do a short **mindfulness activity** before your study session. Tune into your thoughts. Try to observe where your fear of failure is coming from. What is the worst you think can happen?

If the answer comes to you easily, try **writing down** your worst fears. I often do this, because written down a lot of my anxieties look – not to put too fine a point on it – utterly daft. For example, if I can see a friend of mine has read my WhatsApp but hasn't replied, my brain says:

> 'They aren't replying because what you sent them has offended them in some way. You were somehow really insensitive in a way you couldn't have fathomed and are a bad friend. No one really likes you.'

Logically, I know none of this is true. People often read WhatsApp messages on the fly and think 'I'll reply later'. Yet it's only by articulating that thought and giving it oxygen that I can see how ridiculous it is. Acknowledging your fears takes away their power - if you try to squash them your amygdala can think you're ignoring it and scream them even louder to get your attention.

AN EXERCISE FOR PERFECTIONISTS

If you relate to a lot of what I've written above and often find yourself procrastinating because of a fear of failure, try this . . .

- **Get together a group of friends (four or more ideally) and sit in a circle with a piece of paper and a pen in front of each of you.**

- **Write your name at the top of the piece of paper and pass it to your left.**

- **When you receive a piece of paper from the person to your right, write your favourite thing about that person whose name is at the top of the page. Even if you don't know them very well, try to think of something positive about them.**

- **Fold the paper over so that only the name is visible at the top, not what you have written, and pass the paper to the person on your left.**

- **Continue doing this until you receive the paper with your name at the top.**

- **You can then unfold it and see what has been written about you.**

What you will likely discover from doing this exercise is that the reasons why you are **genuinely** valued are very different from the reasons you are usually told you are valued. We spend so much time commenting on each other's grades, possessions, hair or other physical attributes we can forget the real reasons why we choose people as friends.

Of course your grades are important.

But they're not the most important thing about you.

If – and this is a big if – you fail you'll *still* be funny, or brave, or kind or a good listener or any of the other attributes listed on the paper.

> KEEP THE CONCERTINA OF PAPER WITH YOU TO REMIND YOU YOUR WORTH IS MORE THAN A GRADE.

ANXIETY TO-DO LIST

If your head feels as though it's too full to function, you might find it useful to make an anxiety to-do list.

INSTRUCTIONS

1. Take three pieces of paper, preferably in three colours (I like to go traffic-light classic – green, amber and red).

2. At the top of the colour you find most soothing (I choose green) write . . .

PROBLEMS OVER WHICH I HAVE DIRECT CONTROL

3. Now list anything that's troubling you which **you (and only you)** have the power to change.

For example:

I haven't done my homework

I'm hungry

I need to do some exercise/sleep

....

....

4 Now, choose the piece of paper with a colour that's the second most soothing for you (I choose amber) and at the top write . . .

PROBLEMS I NEED SOMEONE ELSE'S HELP WITH

5 List any worries you have which are surmountable but **you need support to get there**[*].

For example:

I've had a week off college sick and I'm now behind on my work

I have a essay question in front of me and it might as well be written in Klingon

I need to borrow some money

....

....

---

[*] **A note on asking for help.** Recent 'wisdom' frames reaching out for support as a sign of 'weakness'. We live in an incredibly individualistic society and this has led to an expectation that we must be capable of handling everything in our lives alone.

However, humans are **tribal animals**. We, physically at least, are totally rubbish compared with, say, a tiger. Therefore, we have historically stood the best chance of survival in packs. From an evolutionary perspective, then, it makes sense that we are born 'flawed' in some way. If human beings were perfect – i.e. strong, clever and skilled enough to survive alone, we'd kill each other (even more than we do already). We have to rely on one another and in order for that to happen we have to have some vulnerabilities.

Therefore, if you ask for help you aren't showing weakness. You are, on a fundamental and evolutionary level, simply **being human**.

55

6 Next to each item on this list, write who you are going to approach to ask for help with that problem.

You may wish to get a **fourth** piece of paper here and draw your network. Write down everyone in your life that might be in a position to give you advice or support. For example, your mum might be great at budgeting, your dad might be really well travelled and therefore good at helping you plan your impending gap year. You might have a really emotionally intelligent friend who is a great listener who you would turn to if you had a friendship issue. You might have another friend who is super smart and loves nothing more than helping other people study. Write down who you know, what their areas of expertise are and you have a document you can refer back to next time you have a problem. It's best to do this immediately – after all, you wouldn't wait until you were falling to start building your safety net.

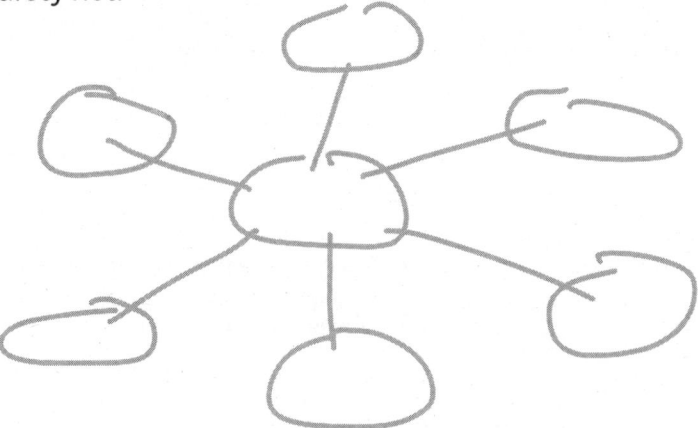

7 Finally, take the piece of paper in the colour you find most aggressive and urgent (I choose red) and write at the top . . .

PROBLEMS I CANNOT CONTROL

For example:

Other people are behaving in ways I don't approve of

There might be World War Three

If I don't get a certain grade I can't get into the university/college/apprenticeship I want to do*

....

....

....

....

....

....

....

* *See overleaf for why this worry belongs on this piece of paper.*

8 ONLY IF YOU CAN DO SO SAFELY, *burn* the red (or whichever colour you have chosen) piece of paper.

If you cannot burn it, **tear it up** into teeny tiny pieces, stamp on it a bit and then throw it in the bin. These are symbolic gestures – **we must let go of what we cannot control.**

Ta daaa! The **two** pieces of paper you are left with are your 'anxiety to-do list', which you can tackle chunk by chunk.

9 You might want to cut each problem into a strip of paper and arrange your problems in order of urgency, or you can number them so you know what to tackle first.

WHY YOUR GRADES SHOULD GO ON THE PIECE OF PAPER YOU THROW AWAY

A lot of people reading this would put their final grade on the green (or most soothing colour) piece of paper, filing it under **'problems over which they have direct control'**. After all, your grade is a reflection of your work and no one can do it for you.

However, your grade is an outcome.

You can, by definition, only do your best. Your homework will be marked by someone else and marked according to assessment criteria you didn't write and therefore the marks you receive could be argued to be completely outside of your control.

I'm not making this argument to disempower you: in fact, quite the opposite. The reason we shouldn't dwell too much on outcomes (like grades) and what they mean for our future is because there is a lot of evidence to show that doing so adversely affects your performance in the task itself.

DRIVING FORCE VS SUPERFICIAL REWARD

The key to motivating yourself to study is to discover your **'driving force'** and then to find a way to make your work closely resemble whatever it is.

WHAT IS MY DRIVING FORCE?

YOUR DRIVING FORCE IS THE REASON YOU GET OUT OF BED IN THE MORNING. BY WHICH I MEAN NOT THE ALARM OF YOUR PHONE, BUT THE THING THAT PUTS FIRE IN YOUR BELLY AND MAKES LIFE WORTH LIVING.

People who know what their driving force is not only tend to give their work their full attention, and therefore achieve more, they're also generally **happier**. Pretty much as soon as we are born, society aggressively tells us what we should be striving for – to make lots of money to buy lots of things to show off.

YET THE FACT IS, HAVING STUFF DOESN'T MAKE YOU HAPPY.

Briefly euphoric, yes, but not truly contented.

Our culture also has a vested interest in persuading us that we should never be content with what we have. After all, people who have enough don't make great consumers and we live in a capitalist society which depends on regular financial transactions to thrive.

If you allow your environment to dictate your motivations, you'll inevitably end up resenting working because your life doesn't really inspire you. Say, for example, your driving force is freedom but you haven't taken the trouble to work that out. You're offered a job with a high salary and long hours and you think 'this is what success looks like, I should take it'. After a few months of never seeing daylight because you're trapped in the office, you're going to end up very dissatisfied, no matter how many zeros are in your pay packet.

A 'SUPERFICIAL REWARD' IS ANYTHING THAT HAPPENS AT THE END OF AN ACHIEVEMENT BUT DOESN'T SERVE YOUR DRIVING FORCE. FOR EXAMPLE, MONEY, LIKES ON SOCIAL MEDIA OR GRADES.

There are a few ways you can discover your driving force . . .

WHAT'S YOUR BIGGEST VALUE?

Think of a time when you were **incandescent with rage** over something which was, objectively, not that important.

We've all been in a situation where our friends are like *'will you STOP going on about such-and-such, it's been three weeks and it didn't matter that much to begin with!'*. When that happens, the chances are whatever happened violated your biggest value. Incidents which breach our values don't have to be objectively significant in order to have a profound impact on us, psychologically.

For example, I once asked a group of fifteen-year-olds if anyone could tell me about a time they had overreacted to something. One of the students gave me what is still my favourite anecdote about **value violation**, if only because the way she told it was funny as hell:

> She'd walked into town after school with her best friend, excited because she had some cash on her (usually she had packed lunch so didn't bring any money into school, but on this occasion for some reason she was buying school lunch, had been given £5 and only spent half of it). After some deliberation, she decided to spend her remaining £2.50 on one of those giant, soft cookies you buy from carts at train stations.
>
> She spent ages selecting her flavour and said she could still remember the feeling of the warmth from the cookie seeping through the bag as she hurried towards a park bench where she could sit down and devour it.

She told her friend so. In fact, she told me about the cookie in quite a lot of reverent detail so we can assume it was a major topic of conversation at the time.

At this point, for no reason whatsoever that she could fathom, her friend decided to stick her leg out, deliberately trip her up so she fell over and dropped her cookie in a puddle. Her friend then proceeded to apologize and claim she didn't know why she did it, all the while laughing uncontrollably.

Our heroine was so upset she turned her back on her friend and 'marched' all the way home in a fit of strop. That, I'd say, is understandable in the circumstances. What followed wouldn't have been out of place as a soap opera storyline. Her friend spent the evening furiously WhatsApping, calling and private messaging her to apologize. She refused to respond. The next day, her friend brought her in a replacement cookie and she threw it in the bin. In the end, she blanked her – lest we forget – BEST friend for three days and, she told me 'I don't really understand why because, at the end of the day, it was a biscuit'.

It **wasn't** just a biscuit, though. It was what the biscuit **represented**. The incident had made our heroine feel daft and had broken a bond of trust. Above all, however, it was **unfair**. Fairness is a key value for some people (and in this particular instance the student in question was a keen campaigner and vocal member of the student council, motivated by wanting to make the world a fairer place).

IF FAIRNESS MOTIVATES YOU, THEN WHATEVER FORM YOUR WORK TAKES, IT MUST SOMEHOW CONTRIBUTE TO ACHIEVING JUSTICE.

WHAT ARE YOUR DESERT ISLAND OBJECTS?

If you were stranded on a desert island and could only pick three objects to take, what would they be?

Now, think about what each object **represents** – chances are, they are a key motivator for you.

For example, lots of people say 'my phone' when I ask them this question. Yet a phone wouldn't get signal on a desert island and logically most people know that. So what does your phone represent to you? For many people, it's connection – the feeling of being constantly plugged into a community.

Belonging is a key psychological human need, so it's little wonder so many of us feel attached to our tribe, whether it's online or IRL. Yet so many of us conduct our study in solitude – that's why we dread it.

WHAT'S YOUR HAPPIEST MEMORY?

Think of the time when you felt most contented (*you know how most of the time we carry around a sense that we're about 3 seconds away from everything descending into unmanageable chaos? The closest you've ever felt to the opposite of that*).

What was happening? Is there anything you can identify as being significant? For example – were you/had you just been on stage? For most people, being on stage is literally the stuff of nightmares, but a certain percentage have a 'performers' mentality'. This means you are driven by attention. HANG ON A MINUTE, I hear you cry, DOESN'T THAT MAKE ME AMONGST THE WORST, MOST ANNOYING PEOPLE ON THE PLANET? Not necessarily (see 'try not to be ashamed of your driving force', page 70).

THE MOST COMMON DRIVING FORCES

Your driving force is **unique to you**. Having said that, there are some common themes and I've listed these here:

ATTENTION
(e.g. performers like **Beyoncé**)

COMPETITION
(e.g. athletes like **Usain Bolt**)

MAKING A DIFFERENCE
(e.g. justice campaigners like **Martin Luther King**)

FREEDOM
(e.g. survivalists like **Bear Grylls**)

SOCIALIZING
(e.g. chat show hosts like **Oprah Winfrey**)

FAIRNESS/ JUSTICE
(e.g. activists like **Malala Yousafzai**)

Make a note of any that apply to you and then try to whittle it down to one that you consider the most important – that's your driving force.

TRY NOT TO BE ASHAMED OF YOUR DRIVING FORCE

'Attention seeker' is a common insult I hear flung around in schools. Whilst I don't agree that it's a helpful label (it's disproportionately used to describe women and most often with the aim of shutting them up) I do understand why 'Look at meeeee!' people can be incredibly annoying.

It's really hard to change what drives you. You can, however, make choices about how you channel your driving force.

An example from my own life. My major motivation is **fairness**. I have a 'comedian's mentality', which means I like to perform to an extent (but only really if I'm making people laugh) but, ultimately, what matters to me most is that the system and the way people behave is fair.

When something is unfair, therefore, no matter how small, it makes me **really angry**. Anger is a necessary emotion, but in its raw form it's rarely helpful. My first instinct is always to take to Twitter and write something along the lines of 'WHY IS EVERYTHING SUCH AN ALMIGHTY MESS?' but that's not going to solve anything. I have therefore learned to **harness** that anger and use it to motivate me to work (because, I figure, when I am Queen of Everything I can ensure that life is absolutely fair).

MAKING YOUR STUDY MATCH YOUR DRIVING FORCE

My mum still talks about my obsession with Cardinal Wolsey when I was doing my A levels. Legend has it that I used to talk to her about him through the crack in the bathroom door whilst she was trying to have a relaxing bath (I neither confirm nor deny the truth of this).

For those unfamiliar, Cardinal Wolsey was a close advisor to Henry VIII. In true Henry VIII style, when Cardinal Wolsey had outlived his usefulness he was executed, having been tried on almost totally fabricated charges. I read outside the required reading on the Tudors, just because I wanted to understand WHY. What were the flaws in the legal system which allowed Henry VIII to get away with such behaviour? What was Wolsey's legacy? Was any kind of relationship with a monarch back then a Faustian pact?

Yep, you guessed it, the story of Cardinal Wolsey had (unbeknownst to me at the time) played into my overwhelming sense that everything should be **fair**.

From what I could glean from my reading, Wolsey was a stand-up bloke with great intentions, his only crime being to stick to his religious and social convictions in the face of Henry VIII constantly changing his policies, owing to thinking with his libido. Hence my thirst to know more.

If you can see the ways in which your study matches your pre-existing internal compass, you'll always find it interesting, if only in a 'means to an end' type way. For example, you might be really into philosophy, but not so much into maths. If you can find a way to think about maths philosophically, it will motivate you to do it. That is easier than it sounds - the universe is made up of numbers and people who study theoretical physics (i.e. really, really fancy maths) are the closest to understanding its secrets. Maths might help you discover the meaning of life (and if it does please email me and tell me what it is).

Here are some other ways to make your study time match your driving force:

I'M A PEOPLE PERSON

If your driving force is being sociable, it makes sense to study in groups. Get some snacks in and make a night of it. However, make sure that your study group contains at least one person who is good at discipline and can ensure you stay on track.

I WANT TO BREAK FREEEEE

Pack your bags and take your books somewhere that feels less restricting than your bedroom. There is literally no law against revising up a tree (unless of course said tree is on private land).

I WANT TO MAKE A DIFFERENCE

Is there someone in your friendship group who struggles with a subject you enjoy? Help them with their study – you're also going over the subject matter, and explaining it to someone else is a great way of helping you remember it.

LOOK AT ME, PLEASE

Teaching is a type of performing. So prepare a 'class' on your chosen topic and present it to your friends. Make it funny and entertaining – it'll help both them and you retain the information.

I'M COMPETITIVE

Start a competition with yourself. Write questions on flashcards and time yourself answering them. Log your times and see if you can beat them. Track any improvements in your grades on a chart (competitive people LOVE charts).

TIMETABLING
BE REALISTIC – AND HONEST

A lot of the students I talk to tell me there 'literally aren't enough hours in the day' for them to do the amount of study they need to. Year 11s and sixth formers often tell me they get home and spend **six hours** on homework and revision every single night, which doesn't even leave them enough time to get the amount of sleep they need. When I speak to their teachers, they tell me this is much more time than the work should take – so why the anomaly?

It's usually because, if they were being entirely honest, the **six hours** that student has spent at their desk (or wherever they're doing their study) hasn't been **completely** dedicated to homework/revision. Do you study with chat windows open? With your phone next to your laptop and notifications turned on? You might not think that the twelve seconds it takes to reply to a message is interfering that much with your study, but it sets you back more than you'd think . . .

Imagine you're a juggler and your thoughts are balls...

Whenever you make a connection between ideas you're introducing another ball into the circle. By the time you're in full problem solving/essay writing mode you have about **six thought balls** in the air.

If you get a message notification and stop to answer it, you **drop** all the balls. Yet, as we know, jugglers can't start from a place of juggling six balls at once. They always begin with two, then introduce a third, then a fourth and so on. So the act of answering the notification doesn't just cost you the time it took to answer it, it's **also** the time it takes to get yourself back into a headspace where you have all six balls in the air.

IF YOU'RE AT SCHOOL OR COLLEGE DURING THE DAY, THE MOST INDEPENDENT STUDY YOU SHOULD BE DOING IN THE EVENING IS 2 HOURS.

Do an experiment: Set yourself 2.5 hours to study and break it up with an activity (see pages 100-123). Agree in advance with your friends that you will be offline for this time. Dedicate yourself to nothing but study and break-time activities for the **two and a half hours** and see how it changes your overall productivity.

You might be so in the habit of checking your phone every few minutes that you find you're 'dropping balls' anyway the first couple of times you try this. Once you're into the swing of it, if you do still genuinely have **much more work** than can be done in your 2.5-hour allotted time period then speak to your teachers – you've been

overloaded.

ARE YOU A LARK OR A NIGHT OWL?

At the weekends, or when you're on **study leave before your exams**, you no longer necessarily need to work just in the evenings. However, it makes sense to plan in advance when your study hours will be lest you develop a 'yay-I've-got-all-day-oh-no-it's-bedtime-and-I-haven't-done-it' routine. One thing that can help you block out your study hours is understanding your natural, internal rhythms.

Some people are **'larks'**, which means they are at their most productive first thing in the morning, others are **'owls'**, meaning they often feel inspired at night time. Others (like me and, uhm, Hitler apparently) are **neither** and actually get most achieved in the middle hours of the day. To find out which you are, take the quick test below:

1 If there were no rules, what time would you choose to wake up?
   A: 6ish
   B: 8ish
   C: 11ish
   D: After 12pm

2 ...And what time would you go to bed?
   A: 8ish
   B: 10ish
   C: Midnight
   D: The wee small hours

3 **How many times to do you press snooze on your alarm in the morning?***
   A: None
   B: Once
   C: Twice
   D: More than twice

4 **Do you think you could wake up without an alarm clock?**
   A: Easy!
   B: Maybe
   C: Probably not
   D: The odds are up there with no one having a social media spat for an entire year

5 **How hungry are you when you first wake up?**
   A: Ravenous
   B: Always in the mood for breakfast
   C: Don't really want anything
   D: Actually feel sick

*A note on pressing **snooze:** when we are awoken from sleep by an alarm it causes a **cortisol spike** (being woken up is fairly stressful, as we all know). Pressing snooze has therefore been shown to increase the quantity of stress chemicals in our systems **before the day has even begun.** It also starts a new sleep cycle (an entire cycle lasts 90 minutes) which could result in us being even more bleary and confused than we would have been if we'd just got up the first time. **Annoying but true.**

6 How chatty are you during the first hour after you wake up?
   A: Can literally jump right back into conversations I was having the previous day
   B: I'm pretty alert and can answer questions people ask me quickly
   C: It doesn't feel like my brain is fully in gear
   D: I am capable only of communicating in grunts (unless it's to tell someone to go away)

7 What time would you choose to do an intense workout?
   A: First thing in the morning
   B: Mid-morning
   C: Afternoon
   D: Last thing before bed

8 And finally, if you had power over what time of day you sat your exams, which would you choose?
   A: 8-10am
   B: 11am-1pm
   C: 2-4pm
   D: 6-8pm

For every A score yourself 4 points
B = 3 points
C = 2 points
D = 1 point

IF YOU SCORED BETWEEN:

24-32: YOU ARE A **LARK**

You're one of those **'morning people'** and are likely to become less energized and functional as the day goes on. Your ideal study hours are between 8 and midday.

Top tip for larks: Get your study space ready the evening before with everything you need to dive straight in the next morning.

16-23: YOU'RE **NEITHER** A LARK NOR AN OWL

There is no name for people like us, so I'm going to call us **seagulls**. (I'm basing this on the fact that you most often see seagulls in the afternoon and **not** because seagulls are quite clearly entitled little buggers who steal your chips.)

Your energy and concentration levels peak in the middle of the day and your ideal study hours are between 11am and 4pm.

Top tip for seagulls: Eating a large meal usually results in a post-lunch energy slump, so divide your lunch into two decent-sized snacks and space them out, instead.

8-16: YOU'RE A NIGHT OWL

Anyone who talks to you in the morning is going to get short shrift because you just don't feel human until about **midday.** However, you're often struck by great ideas in the evening and are happy to work at night. Your ideal study time is 6-10pm.

Top tip for owls: In fact, owing to biological changes which happen during this phase of your life, **most** teenagers are owls. However, most fun social things also happen in the evenings. If you're on study leave, make a pact with other owls that you'll get together and do something fun during the day (cinemas tend to be blissfully empty at this time) so you don't feel like you're missing out.

STUDY TIPS

INCORPORATE AS MANY OF THE **FIVE SENSES** AS YOU CAN INTO REVISION.

SIGHT

Most people now learn about **mind maps** at school as a matter of course, but I was introduced to them via an obscure VHS my mum found . . . actually I don't know where she found it . . . but it *totally* changed my approach to revision.

Mind maps use a combination of **images** and **words** in a colourful spider-diagram type format to summarize key information. They work because when you read a word your brain 'hears it'. Words are therefore an *audio*, as opposed to a *visual*, cue. By using images and colours, we give the brain more than one metaphorical 'peg' on which to hang the information and are therefore able to recall it more easily.

A MIND MAP OF REVISION TECHNIQUES

Write the word **revision** or draw something that represents revision - like a pile of books - at the centre of your piece of paper.

Draw branches representing each section of this chapter coming out from the centre. Each branch should be a different colour. Label them - motivation, study time, procrastination, senses, breaks.

Draw smaller branches coming out of the big branches with a word or picture representing what you have learned about yourself during each section - for example, an owl, an alarm clock showing 6pm (the best time to start study for a night owl) and the third with a picture of a ticket stub to represent seeing a film with your friends during the day.

You can use this technique to map out the areas of study for each subject.

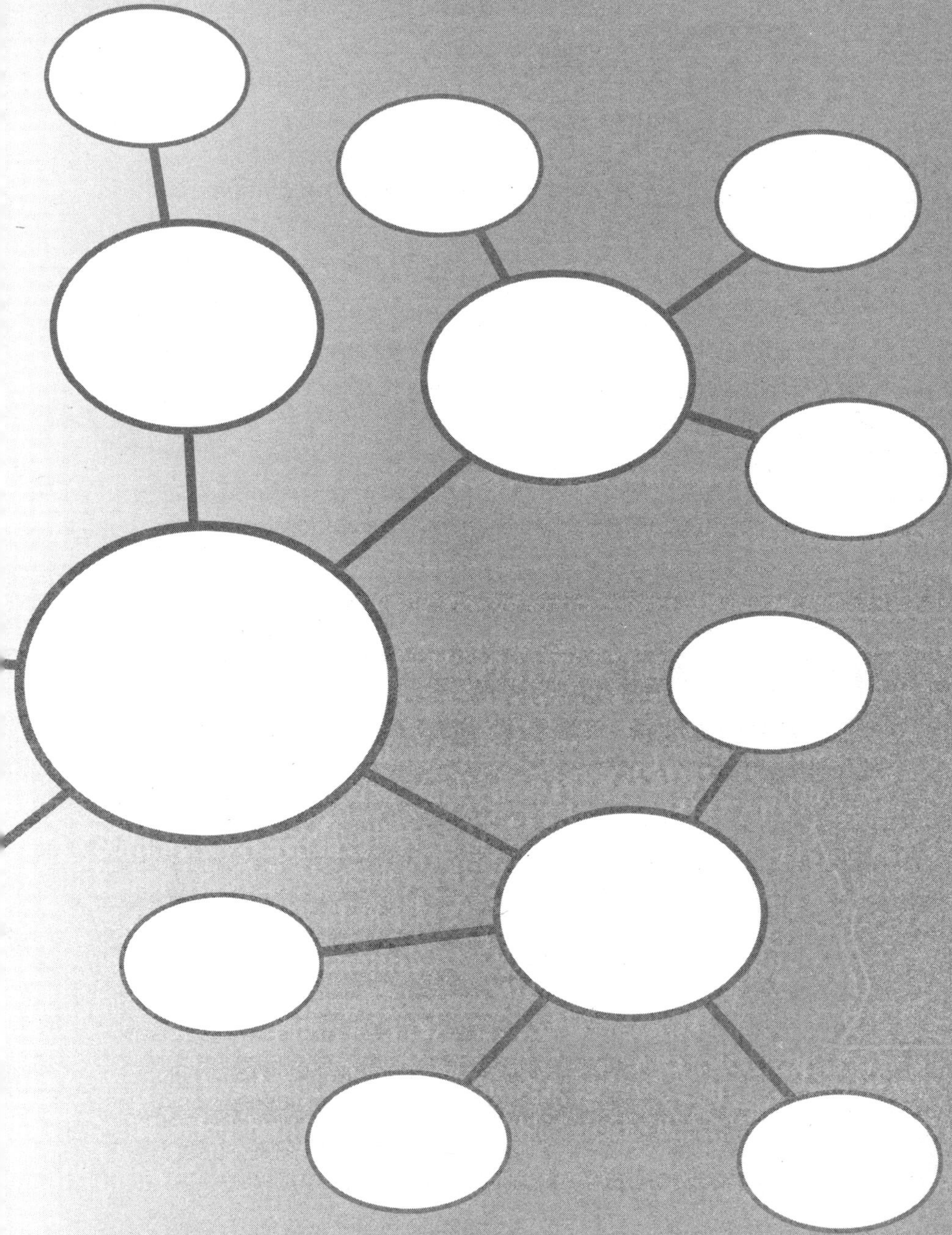

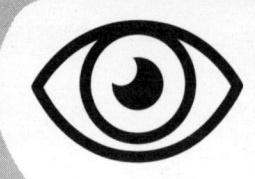

SIGHT

You can also stick up pictures of relevant historical figures or maps or a list of quotes to create visual recall cues.

SMELL

Some people swear by using smell to similar effect – although it has to be a fragrance you could recreate in an exam hall. Try putting a distinct brand of body spray or perfume on whilst revising, then spray it again the next day in an unrelated situation and see if it brings back any of the information.

HEARING 1: TELL STORIES

The human brain LOVES a narrative. We are a species of story-tellers and, throughout our evolution, this was how tribal elders passed down vital information to their children and grandchildren, which would allow them to survive and flourish.

We're therefore wired to remember information more easily if it's in the form of a story. It doesn't have to be particularly sophisticated.

I use this all the time when remembering people's names. So, for example, I recently met an amazing guy called Gulwali, which is pronounced like 'Ruali'. To remember that, I thought of Ru Paul talking to a pirate called Lee. Ru – ARRRR – Lee. (WELCOME TO MY BRAIN, EVERYONE.)

HEARING 2: SING IT

You know how you can remember all the lyrics to a song you don't even particularly like, but mathematical formulas just won't stay in your head in the same way (annoyingly)? It's because tunes help us remember words. Put a melody to your revision. Make it a song you already know and if you find yourself going blank in the exam, you can remember the tune to (hopefully) bring back the content.

TOUCH

If you don't have to wear a uniform for your exam, trying putting on a garment with a specific texture – like a shirt with a ribbon at the cuff, or a T-shirt with a raised slogan on the front. Touch the silk or the raised letters as you recall a key fact. You might find fiddling in the same way during the exam causes you to recall that fact.

TASTE

You're not allowed to eat or chew in the exam hall, but you could try eating foods with a strong aftertaste – like aniseed or mint – whilst revising and then eating a sweet with the same flavour just prior to your exam.

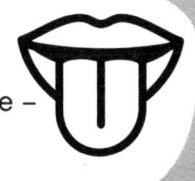

PUT REMINDERS IN UNEXPECTED LOCATIONS

Write notes or select images from your mindmaps on Post-its and put them in places your brain **doesn't** associate with revision, like the bathroom mirror and the fridge door. Your mind's capacity for thought is 90% unconscious, which means even if you don't actively register them, you'll still absorb them instinctually as you pass them each day.

MAKE YOUR REVISION LOOK LIKE BOOBS

Your recall is highest at the beginning and end of any one period of concentration. Let's say you had an hour to revise – that means your ability to remember would peak for the first and last few minutes of that hour. If drawn, your concentration would look like this:

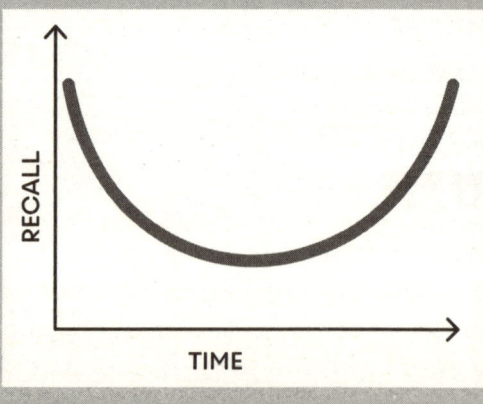

If, however, you choose to divide the hour into **two shorter periods** of 25 minutes with a ten-minute break in between, you double the amount of time your recall peaks, meaning you recall more information. In this instance, your concentration looks like boobs:

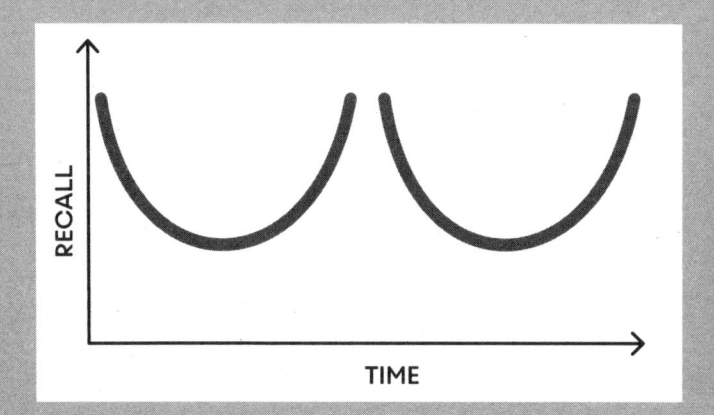

There's a balance to be struck here, since we know interruptions cause you to **'drop'** the intellectual balls you are juggling. A reasonable goal would be to ensure you spend **half an hour** – which you can divide into breaks of **ten** or **twenty** minutes – away from your books during any one period of study.

I'm sure you can already see where I'm going with this: the ultimate aim is to spend those ten- or twenty-minute breaks doing endorphin-releasing activities which counteract cortisol and adrenaline in the system and restore chemical balance – that way, you're not only optimizing your ability to revise but also improving your mental fitness simultaneously: WIN.

In the next section you'll find suggestions for short activities you can do to break up study sessions . . .

SECTION 3
PREPARATION AND TIME MANAGEMENT

WE KNOW from Section 2 that there are certain activities which are currently **keeping you sane** and the worst thing you could do would be to sacrifice them to study. An effective work plan therefore takes these wellbeing-promoting activities and...

PLANS STUDY TIME AROUND THOSE, RATHER THAN THE OTHER WAY AROUND.

Below you'll find suggestions of 10, 20 and 30 minute activities you can use to **break up** study sessions, along with expert tips.

First, though, think about your current study environment and home-from-school routine.

YOUR BEDROOM

Most people study in their bedrooms. However, we also know how important sleep is to maintaining good mental health. Sleep experts say ideally your bedroom should be a **sanctuary** from the rest of the world and you wouldn't do anything in it but sleep.

If you have the space, try to **cordon off** a section of your bedroom specifically for studying. Try not to let things like text books out of your 'study zone'. If that's just not possible, then make sure you put your laptop, books, mind maps and anything else you associate with schoolwork into a pile and **out of your eyeline** as part of your 'winding down for bed' routine.

I have always found it really difficult to work in a messy room. If you relate, but also don't want to spend valuable study time wielding a feather duster, here's a few simple things that don't take long but give the impression of a tidy room:

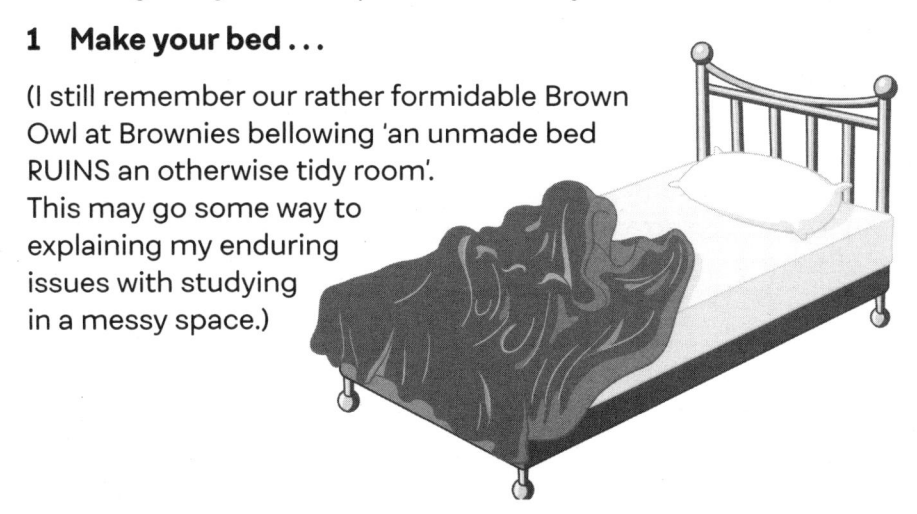

1   Make your bed...

(I still remember our rather formidable Brown Owl at Brownies bellowing 'an unmade bed RUINS an otherwise tidy room'. This may go some way to explaining my enduring issues with studying in a messy space.)

If you can't be bothered to make your bed properly, lift up and shake out your duvet. A smooth duvet gives the impression of a tidy bed. This is also a great move for working out your biceps.

2 Get storage boxes...

You can get inexpensive ones online. Shoving your mess into a box takes all of about three seconds and gives a pleasing impression of tidiness.

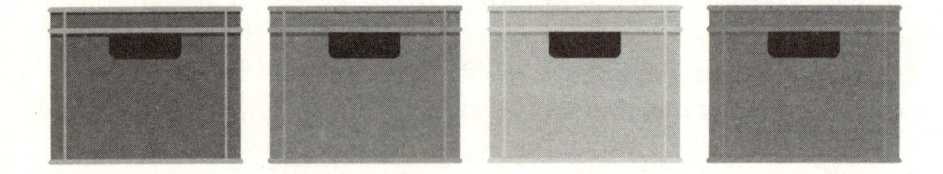

3 Hang up your clothes or put them in the laundry basket

I know it doesn't seem like a big deal to have the odd pair of pants scattered here and there but (assuming – or rather hoping – you change your pants daily) it doesn't take long to accumulate a giant and potentially distracting pant mountain.

OTHER TIPS YOU MIGHT FIND USEFUL

- Make sure your study space is the right temperature – too cold and you won't be able to concentrate, too hot and you'll fall asleep.

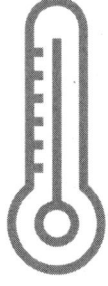

- Crack open a window – fresh air helps you concentrate.

- Make sure you have everything you need before you start work (i.e. pens, highlighters, blank paper, text books).

- Staying hydrated is important – keep a glass of water nearby.

CREATE YOUR 'HOME TO STUDY' ROUTINE

Eighteenth-century wisdom tells us 'procrastination is the thief of time'. Despite this, it is not a good idea to get straight home from school, sprint to your room and start on homework. Try to create a routine based around the following three things:

1: 'DUMP'

It's important to have an outlet for anything that has excited/frustrated you during the course of the day. If you have the sort of relationship that allows you do so, talking to your parents or siblings is an excellent way to do this. Explain to them in advance that you aren't necessarily looking for advice or solutions, it just helps you to go 'BLAH' at someone and offload the events of the day.

If you suspect your parent or sibling would be amenable to this but have **no idea** how to go about having the conversation, try approaching it with a consistent metric.

- **Rate** your day from **1** to **7** (1 being a catastrophic disaster, 7 being Michelle Obama visited your school and gave everyone unlimited free chocolate, or similar).
- Is this score **lower** or **higher** than yesterday? If so, what happened to bring the number up or down?
- What was the **highlight** of your day?
- What would need to happen to ensure your score was **higher** (or if 7, the same) tomorrow?

Try to get into the habit of answering these four questions daily. If you can't talk to any of the humans in your household but have pets, try telling them (dogs are excellent listeners). If you don't feel comfortable articulating the answers aloud then **write them down**.

THIS EXERCISE ALLOWS YOU TO **'DUMP'** ANY EMOTIONAL BAGGAGE YOU HAVE BROUGHT HOME WITH YOU.

2: CHANGE

School uniforms are usually made of horrendously **itchy** man-made fibres and seemingly designed in such a way as to ensure you remain as uncomfortable as possible throughout the day.

BEFORE YOU START STUDYING, CHANGE INTO YOUR 'COMFIES'. I FAVOUR A PAIR OF JOGGERS OR PYJAMA BOTTOMS AND A LOOSE (USUALLY DAVID BOWIE-THEMED) T-SHIRT WHEN I'M WORKING FROM HOME, BUT THAT'S ONLY BECAUSE I'M **TOO TALL FOR ONESIES.**

3: REFUEL

Eat something that is going to sustain you until dinner. Bananas are an excellent choice for a quick energy boost, along with nuts and/or seeds, which are surprisingly filling and a good source of protein. Try to avoid anything that's going to cause a sugar or caffeine crash, such as energy drinks – you might get a slight temporary buzz but you'll be face down asleep in a text book within an hour.

If you prefer to have a snack to hand whilst you're working, blueberries are apparently good brain fuel and are the handy sort of thing you can decant into a bowl.

HOW MUCH TIME SHOULD I SPEND STUDYING?

YOUR TEACHERS will be able to give you guidance on the right amount of time to spend doing homework or revision after school or college. No teacher I've ever met has recommended going over **2 hours per night**. If you are genuinely spending that time working (and not answering notifications, as explored in Section 2) that should be enough time to do whatever you need to do.

If you are intending to spend two hours studying, break up the session to keep up your productivity levels. You should aim for a total **half an hour** break regardless of the amount of time you intend to study.

There are a few ways you can do this:

1 hour study • 30-minute activity • 1 hour study

40-minute study • 20-minute activity • 40-minute study • 10-minute activity • 40-minute study

30-minute study • 10-minute activity • 30-minute study • 10-minute activity • 30-minute study • 10-minute activity • 30-minute study

Whichever way you choose to break up your study time, the total amount of time for study and break is 2.5 hours.

ACTIVITY IDEAS

10-MINUTE ACTIVITIES

SKIP

That's right, with a rope, like you did when you were five. Skipping is used in the training of many professional athletes because it's amazing at getting your heart rate up and keeping you fit. It's also completely knackering so should be done in short bursts.

FREEWRITING

Choose a topic – it doesn't matter how random – it can be anything from your favourite film to the lifecycle of frogspawn. Whatever grabs your imagination that day. Then, for ten minutes, write continuously with that topic in mind. It doesn't matter if what comes onto the page is nonsense . . . In fact, that's kinda the point. Freewriting gives you a glimpse into the freaky world of your subconscious.

START A STORY

Type a paragraph of a story – it doesn't matter how daft the premise – then email it to a friend and ask them to write the next paragraph. You can do this as a group so that whoever you sent it to adds their contribution then forwards it to a third person and so on, or you can ping pong between each other. The trick is to be disciplined and limit to one paragraph per day.

GET SOME FRESH AIR

Fresh air really does help clear the mind. If you have a garden, go for a wander round it. If you live in a flat and have a balcony, stand on it and take some deep, relaxing breaths for a few minutes (see below). Even sticking your head out of the window for a bit will help you feel rejuvenated.

BREATHE

Most of us assume we're rather good at breathing, since we've been doing it consistently since we were born. But anxiety and stress can often cause shallow breathing or hyperventilating, which makes us feel even worse. Take a few minutes to focus on taking long, deep breaths – inhale through your nose for a count of seven and then exhale for a count of ten. See how long you can maintain this for – it isn't easy, but 7 or 8 minutes of doing this is enough to achieve serious levels of chill.

MAKE A CUP OF TEA

Note: You will get brownie points if you ask your parents if they want one, too.

WOZZLE AN ANIMAL

If you have a pet, spend a few minutes stroking (or 'wozzling' as it's known in our house) or playing with them. There's a lot of evidence to show that animals are magic for our wellbeing. Stroking them releases oxytocin – a feel-good chemical. It is, I believe, physically impossible to be in a bad mood within three feet of a dog. A study by the Mental Health Foundation found that 87% of people who own a cat said it had had a positive impact on their wellbeing.

STRETCH

Spending a lot of time focusing on study often means our posture suffers. This can in turn cause aches, pains and a general feeling of 'blah'. Taking ten minutes to do a few basic stretches will realign your body for the next section of study. Try the simple techniques below:

Stand tall with your feet together and your hands at chest level, fingers woven together. Turn your palms

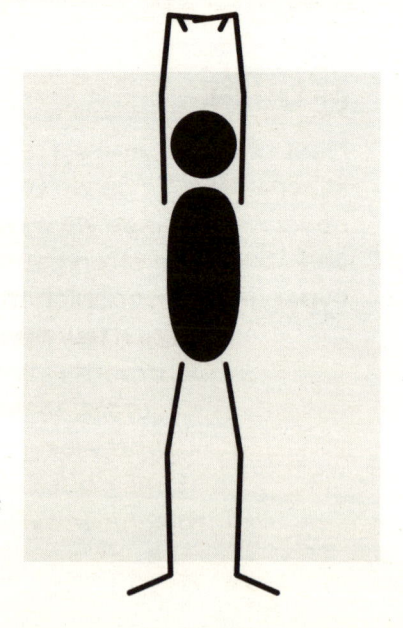

away from you and lift your hands as high as you can above your head. With your neck relaxed, stretch your arms and torso and stand on tiptoe. Hold for a slow count of five.

Stand with your feet hip width apart. Bend from the waist and get your chest as close to your thighs as you can. Hang out there for a slow count of ten. See if you can get your palms flat on the floor (it might take a few goes but the more you stretch the more flexible you become, so give it time).

SING

According to the Sing Up Foundation, singing naturally lowers the amount of cortisol in your system and therefore lowers stress. Neuroscientists have also found that when we sing, the right temporal lobe of our brain lights up, which in turn causes endorphin production. There's a great site I use – **www.karaoke-version.co.uk** – you can find instrumental versions of thousands of songs on there. (I do sometimes have to bribe my neighbours with wine if I'm planning a night of singing Queen's greatest hits, but it's totally worth it).

20-MINUTE ACTIVITIES

CARTOONIZE YOURSELF

Try creating a cartoon version of yourself. If you get really good, you can have your cartoon self in all kinds of positions and scenarios and create a comic strip, or post them online. The illustrations in this book are by Ruby Elliot, better known as Rubyetc. I asked her for some tips for beginners:

NEVER WENT TO ART SCHOOL

HASN'T DRAWN SINCE THEY WERE A KID

① EARS

② FELINE ACCESSORIES

③ SWIRL IT ROUND

④ TA-DAH!

Don't Overthink it...
Art is just mark making and something that everyone can enjoy regardless of technical ability. Don't overthink it when you draw. Worry less about things looking perfect and more on the enjoyment and silliness of the process.

TODAY I FEEL LIKE...

A HUMMINGBIRD THAT CAN'T STOP FLAPPING ITS WINGS

A BIG MESSY LUMP IN FANCY SHOES

AN ICE CREAM THAT HAS BEEN LEFT OUT TOO LONG AND IS ALL MELTY AND RIDICULOUS

Be Bold...
Go straight in with pen, see what it feels like to not cross or rub things out! Draw from reference/photos of yourself if that's easier, but if you're not confident then focus on basic shapes and lines to say as much as you can with as little as possible.

Forget Realism...
It doesn't have to be detailed or realistic, your version of you could be as simple as a blob with hair labelled "me", or perhaps a big scribbly mess if that's what you feel like. When creating a character, pick 1-3 essential features or feelings you want to convey and focus on those (much easier than spending 2 hours trying to shade in a nostril).

AND FINALLY...

**Remember that artistic licence is real;
the page really is yours to do what you want with!**

LISTEN TO A TED TALK

TED ask inspirational speakers from the worlds of science, technology, business and creativity to talk on a subject they're passionate about. If you go to **www.ted.com** you can type in your interests and the website will suggest a talk for you. The quality of TED talks is generally really high and some **magnificent** brains have taken part – it's almost impossible to listen to one and not emerge motivated as hell. Here are a few of my favourites:

> **Brené Brown** – 'The Power of Vulnerability'
>
> **Anil Seth** – 'Your brain hallucinates your conscious reality'
>
> **Caroline Casey** – 'Looking past limits'
>
> **Hannah Gadsby** – 'Three ideas. Three contradictions. Or not'
>
> **Sir Ken Robinson** – 'Do schools kill creativity?'

DO SOME YOGA

Important: Before beginning yoga, it's essential that you think about any physical injuries or disabilities you might have that might make the activity dangerous for you. If in doubt, ask your doctor. Yoga can be a great way to feel better, in mind and in body, but pay attention to how it feels and stop if it hurts.

It's advisable, although not compulsory, to get yourself a yoga mat – most roll up so they can be stored away in the corner of the room when you're not using them. You can be wearing anything that's comfy and that allows you to be flexible.

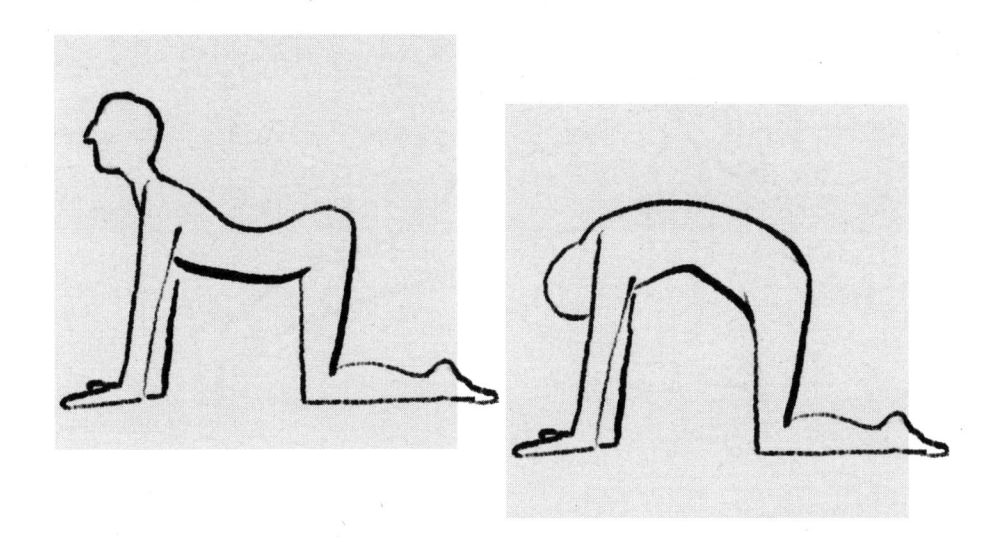

SEQUENCE 1: COW AND CAT

1 Get on your hands and knees with your palms on the floor. Your hands should be aligned with your shoulders and your knees with your hips.

2 Breathe in. As you do so lift your chin and your chest and push your stomach towards the floor so your spine is making a 'U' shape. This is 'cow' (apparently. No idea why as I've never seen a cow do this).

3 Now exhale. As you do so, drop your chin and reverse the shape of your spine so your back is rounded and your belly is sucked in. This is 'cat'*.

4 Repeat this four or five times. Make sure your movement is in time to your breaths, which you should keep slow and relaxed.

If you ever see a cat raise it's back like this in real life it means it's really cheesed off and you should probably run away.

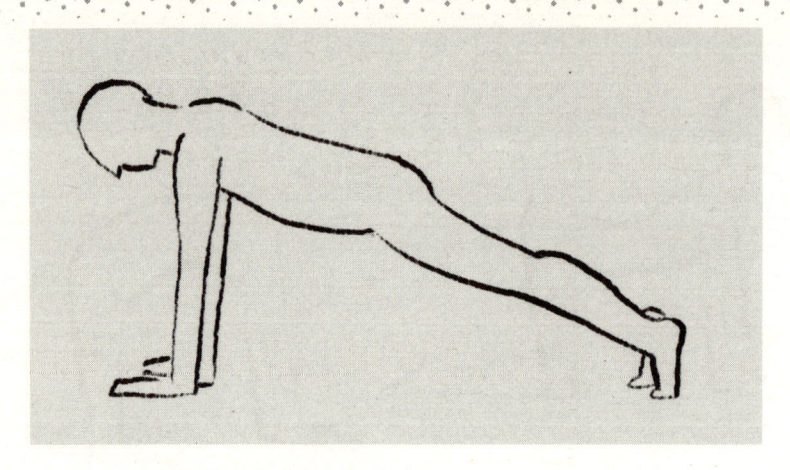

SEQUENCE 2: PLANK

There's about a gazillion YouTube videos of various people planking (it apparently works every muscle in your body) but if you don't want to look because of the smugness, instructions are below:

1. Start on your hands and knees. Step both feet back so you're balancing on the balls of your feet. Keep your legs hip-width apart, your hands aligned with your shoulders and your arms straight (but don't lock your elbows).

2. The reason this move is called a 'plank' is because the aim is to create a straight line from your feet all the way to your head. Try not to let your head drop. Keep it lifted to maintain the plank.

3. Keeping as still as you can, try to take five deep breaths. It's *much* harder than it looks.

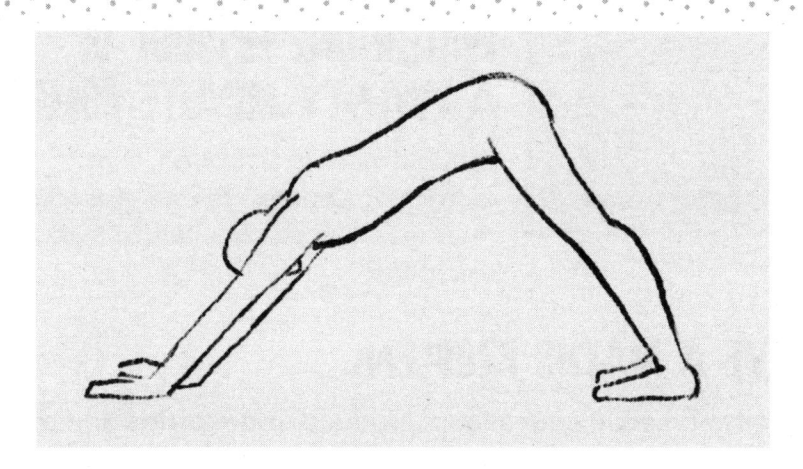

SEQUENCE 3: DOWNWARD FACING DOG

1. From plank pose, exhale and lift your bum to the ceiling – you are aiming to make a triangle shape with your body.

2. Look between your arms and towards your knees, and concentrate on pushing your hands and heels towards the floor. At first, you'll probably find your heels are lifted, but just point them in the right direction and focus and eventually you'll be bendy enough for them to be flat.

3. Try to distribute evenly the weight between your hands and your feet.

4. Try to take five deep, slow, breaths. This is 'downward facing dog' pose. When you are ready, come back down onto your hands and knees.

You can put these three movements together into a routine (it's what I do and I feel very centred and, well, stretched afterwards) and see if you can repeat for 15 minutes.

WATCH ONE EPISODE OF A TWENTY-MINUTE COMEDY

I should warn you though, that restricting yourself to one episode requires Dalai Lama levels of self-discipline.

SOLVE A MATHS PROBLEM

We know creative endeavours produce **endorphins** and that these are crucial to maintaining the brain's optimum chemical balance, ridding us of the adrenaline and cortisol which can impede our academic performance and play havoc with our mental health. Most of us think of activities like drawing, painting, drama and dance as being 'creative' and whilst these are fantastic endorphin producers, a creative activity is really anything which gets the **cogs of your brain whirring** in a non-linear, probably unfamiliar way. Maths problems can be an incredibly creative pursuit, if that's what ices your cupcake.

As mentioned in the previous chapter, I managed to motivate myself to pass my maths GCSE by figuring it might help me discover the meaning behind the universe and all its living creatures. This was a very effective short-term strategy and I did **much better** than anyone, least of all me, expected. Then at A level I discovered philosophy (i.e. chatting about the meaning of life in a numberless and therefore infinitely more fun fashion) and later people like Stephen Hawking and Professor Brian Cox (who had already done the maths for me). So maths and I parted ways when I was 16 and I really only use it now for convincing myself I'm actually saving money when I buy clothes I don't need in the sales.

Luckily, I am friends with Rachel Riley (of Channel 4's *Countdown*) who has a brain unrivalled (certainly amongst my acquaintances) in its mathsiness. Rachel studied mathematics at Oxford University and can often be found saying things like *'if this question doesn't have an answer I can find using an equation then I don't want to discuss it'*.

I asked Rachel what she uses to chill her giant noggin and she pointed me towards **@CShearer41**, the Twitter account of Catriona Shearer, who regularly posts 'fun' maths puzzles (usually resulting in a Twitter spat regarding which of her followers has the correct solution, or has arrived at the solution in the correct way, because of course everything on Twitter must end in a spat).

Here are four of Rachel's favourites, which Catriona gave me permission to reproduce in this book. Apparently, they each take about 20 minutes to solve. If you have a query about any of them ask Rachel (**@RachelRileyRR**) or Catriona because they might as well be hieroglyphics as far as I'm concerned...

The area where these two quarter circles overlap is 16. What's the total shaded area?

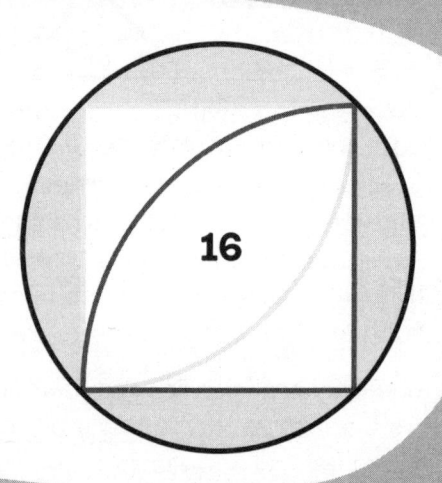

16

The black line, of length 2, is perpendicular to the bases of the three semicircles. What's the total shaded area?

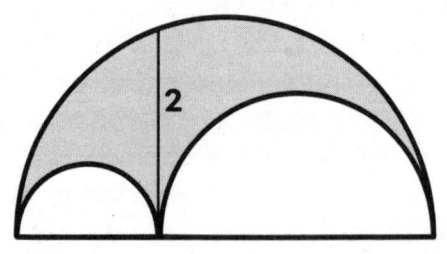

2

If the radius of each semicircle is 5, what's the total shaded area?

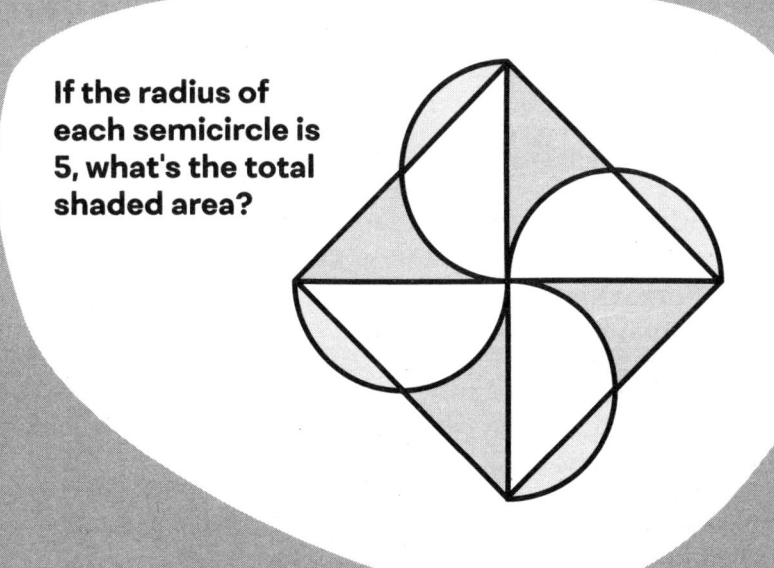

The four dots are equally spaced. What's the total shaded area?

2

113

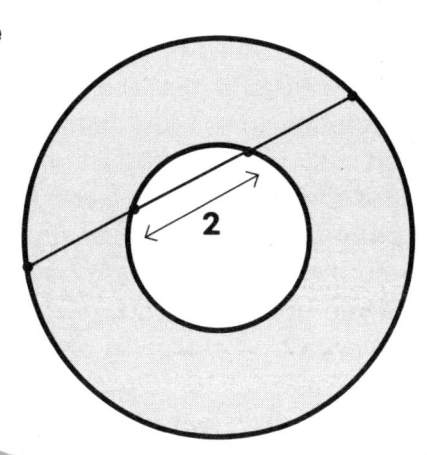

top-left: 16; bottom-left: π;
top-right: 100; bottom-right: 8π

30-MINUTE ACTIVITIES

LISTEN TO A PODCAST

In 2019, **podcastinsights.com** reported that there were over 800,000 podcast brands out there on the net. Whatever your interests, chances are there's a podcast for you.

Podcasts are great because, after a while, you start to feel as though the presenters are your friends but, crucially, there's no obligation to participate in the conversation and it goes on for a finite length of time.

If you're looking for some inspiration to get you started, below are some of my favourite podcasts:

> **No Such Thing As a Fish**
> You know that show *QI* that was hosted by Stephen Fry? NSTAAF is the researchers from that show recounting the four favourite facts they've learned that week. It's totally random, usually hilarious and engaging in a way that doesn't require you to think too hard. (Incidentally – my favourite fact from the series is that the biggest penis ever recorded is only two inches smaller than the world's smallest man.)

Standard Issue

You know lovely, brilliant Sarah Millican the comedian? Well, in December 2014 she started an online publication called 'Standard Issue' as an antidote to all the fat-shamey, 'lipsticky rubbish' she was used to seeing in women's magazines. Unfortunately, advertisers tend not to want to invest in magazines which don't actively reduce people's self-esteem and it went bust.

Determined not to be defeated, the team created the Standard Issue podcast or 'a magazine for your ears'. It's topical, funny, thought-provoking and inspiring too – it will introduce you to lots of brilliant people doing incredible things.

The Guilty Feminist

Ever had one of those days where you're like 'I'm a feminist so why am I hugging myself because someone told me I looked sexy in my last selfie?' If so, this is the podcast for you.

Every week Deborah Francis-White (who should actually be in charge of everything in the world) and a comedian co-host explore 'our noble goals as feminists and the hypocrisies and insecurities which undermine them' with expert (and incredibly diverse) guests. It's recorded in front of a live audience and Deborah and her co-host also do a spot of stand-up on the week's theme.

Richard Herring's Leicester Square Theatre Podcast

Comedian Richard Herring interviews a variety of famous guests in his own unique way: by asking really daft (but highly entertaining) questions such as 'if you had to choose between a hand made of ham or an armpit that could dispense sun cream, which would you pick?'. My favourite interviews are with Louis Theroux and David Mitchell because they're both really deadpan, which makes Richard Herring's schoolboy-esque cheekiness even funnier.

Fact or Bull

Full disclosure: this is **my** podcast. BUT even if it wasn't I reckon I'd choose to listen to it (unbiased, totally objective statement).

Every week, myself and Dr Keon West (social psychologist at Goldsmiths University) take a statement a lot of people believe and discuss with an expert whether it's fact or bull. Examples include: Gender is a social construct; being fat is automatically bad for your health; and there is such a thing as an addictive personality.

Quick note: As someone who makes a podcast, I cannot emphasize enough how much difference it makes when listeners subscribe – it means we're more likely to be able to make more episodes because advertisers will see we are popular. So if you like a podcast and want it to continue, please don't ignore the bit at the end where the presenters wang on about subscribing, rating and leaving a review.

BAKE SCONES

I'm rubbish at baking. It's because it usually requires a lot of measuring and precision, whereas I'm much more of a *'throw it all in the pan and let's see what comes out'* type of cook. So, I am therefore in a position to be able to tell you conclusively that the following scone recipe is foolproof.

You will need: 350g (12oz) of self-raising flour, a pinch of salt, a teaspoon of baking powder, 85g (3oz) of cold butter cut into cubes, 3 tablespoons of caster sugar, 125ml (4 fl oz) milk and an egg.

1. Preheat your oven to 200°C or gas mark 7.

2. Put the self-raising flour into a large bowl (recipe books will tell you to sift it but I can never be arsed and it turns out fine).

3. Add a pinch of salt and a teaspoon of baking powder and (carefully, because flour goes everywhere) mix it all together.

4. Rub the butter into the flour, salt and baking powder using your fingers until it gets all crumby. Try to make sure there are no large chunks of butter left in the mixture.

5. Add three tablespoons of caster sugar and stir until it's evenly distributed.

6. Add 100ml (3.5 fl oz) of milk and stir in quickly using a table knife until it forms a soft dough. Add a little more milk if necessary.

7. Sprinkle some flour onto a clean kitchen surface, tip the dough out of the bowl and sort of flop it about a bit so it gets coated in the flour and takes on a firmer consistency.

8. Pat your dough out until it's about 3-4cm thick then use a 5cm diameter cookie cutter to create as many rounds as you can.

9. Pop the rounds on some greaseproof paper on a baking tray.

10. Crack an egg into a bowl and beat it with a fork, then brush each round with the beaten egg (this bit is SOOOO fun, I find, like glazing pottery).

11. Bake for 12 minutes until risen and golden in colour. The scones are best eaten on the day you bake them. Slice them in half and spread them with butter, cream, jam, or anything else you might fancy.

Tip: NEVER get into a conversation with a person from either Devon or Cornwall on whether you should put the jam or the cream on the scone first. You'll be there all day.

GO FOR A WALK

The philosopher Hippocrates famously said 'walking is the best medicine' (although, in fairness, antibiotics hadn't been invented yet). A brisk walk (fast enough to raise your pulse but slow enough that you could still maintain a conversation) releases endorphins, helps keep your heart healthy, strengthens your bones and helps promote a good night's sleep. And it costs nothing. What's not to love?

READ AN ARTICLE

There's a brilliant website called 'The Mix' (**www.themix.org.uk**) which has a huge archive of genuinely useful articles on relationships, body image worries, money and much more. Or, if you're looking for something a bit more light and entertaining, Buzzfeed never disappoints.

Tip: It's easy to get caught up in a click-cycle because websites put related content at the bottom of their articles. Set a 30-minute timer on your phone to alert you when your browsing time is up.

CREATE YOUR OWN DANCE ROUTINE

Now, obviously half an hour generally isn't enough time to create really elaborate choreography, but it is enough to create a simple routine you can build upon and practise.

Most people I know love to dance, but hardly anyone thinks they're good at it (and the ones that do usually need to CALM DOWN a little bit). My friend Pasha was one of the professional dancers on *Strictly Come Dancing* between 2011 and 2018 and also appeared on *Dancing with the Stars* in the US. As I type he holds the record for the highest average score ever on *Strictly* with his most recent dance partner Ashley Roberts, of Pussycat Dolls fame. He gives some tips below:

It's all about the track . . .
Decide on the music you're going to be dancing to first – your body is there to express what you hear. Play the track once and just see what you feel the urge to do. Anything that's particularly good can form the basis of your routine.

The moonwalk is easier than it looks . . .
If you want to do a step that looks really impressive but is actually quite simple, try the moonwalk. It takes a little time to master but it's really all about knowing which foot to keep flat, which heel to raise and getting the rhythm right between the two.

Whichever foot is moving should be flat and the other heel should be raised. So, if your right leg is moving keep your right foot to the floor and lift your left heel. When the right foot touches the left foot the left leg starts moving – that's when you flatten the left foot and lift up your right heel. You can do this on the spot at first until you have the co-ordination between your feet and then eventually take it into a moving step.

You don't need a great big giant studio . . .
You don't need to make big moves to be able to convey a lot of emotion, and that's really what dance is about. Dance is the ability to listen to a song and choreograph to the rhythm and accents within that song to create a signature of movement. A roll of your eyes can actually be a very strong choreographic move if you choose the right beat to do it in. The other move which always looks dramatic is the 'power grab' – when people sing ballads they often reach forward and squish their fingers into a fist as though grabbing the air – that doesn't require much space but conveys a lot.

Record yourself . . .
Set up your phone on a flat surface so you can record yourself. Look back on the video to see how the way you thought you were moving relates to how it looked in reality. If you think you can tweak it to make it better then try recording yourself again until you are satisfied with what you see.

Don't think you have to look like a stereotypical 'athlete' . . .
A lot of people will tell you this is true. For example, in Latin dancing (which is what I do) you hear people say tall people look 'clunky' doing the moves because they have long arms and legs. Yet I have seen world champions who are tall and have still found a way to co-ordinate themselves as a dancer. Also, one of my favourite dancers does swing, which is a really fast dance and he's a very big guy. But he is able to create the proper frame for his partner and has great rhythm, so it works.

Be aware of your body and what you might have to put extra work into or compensate for but, ultimately, don't let it put you off trying any type of dance. There might be a long line of people who looked a certain way doing one type of dance, but you might be the person who ends up changing the stereotype!

ARE THERE ENOUGH HOURS IN THE DAY?

A few weeks ago I was in a school talking to sixth formers about the importance of making time to **empty their stress buckets** and get enough sleep. One student raised her hand and asked how she was **ever** meant to find enough hours in that day to do all of those things.

Assuming your school or college lets out around 3.30 and most people are home by 4.30, that means:

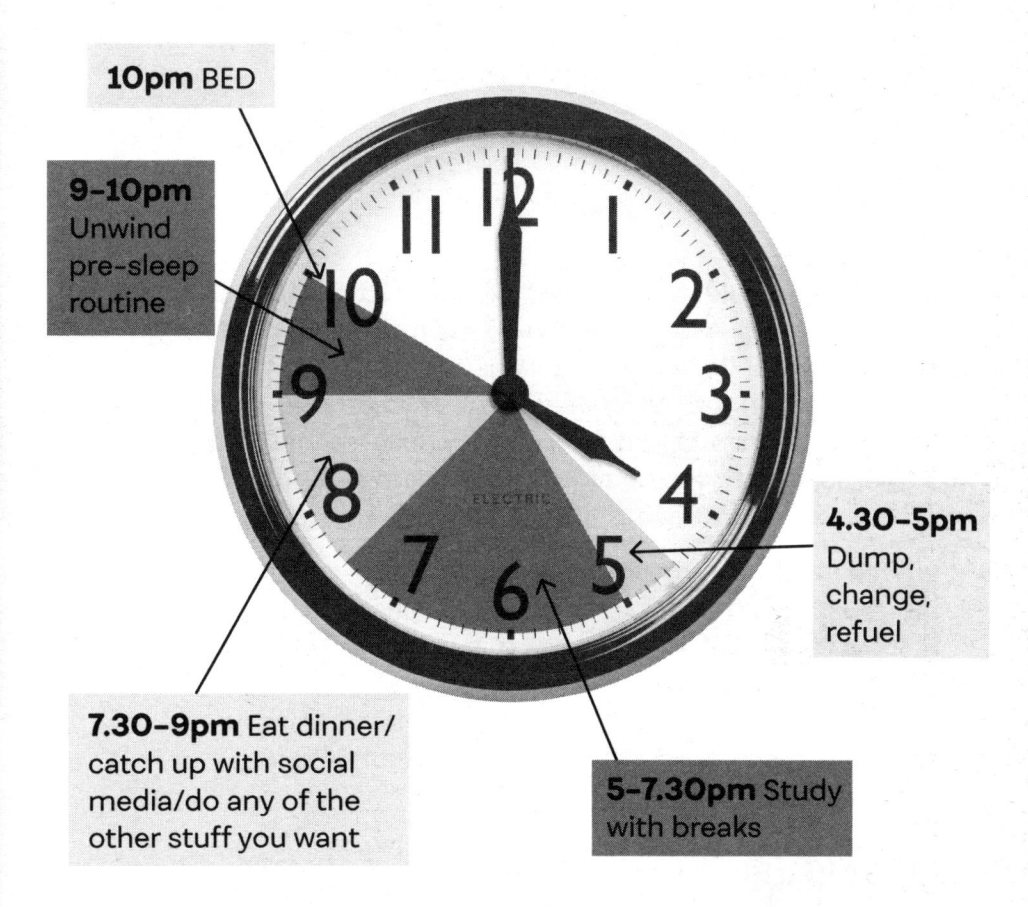

10pm BED

9–10pm Unwind pre-sleep routine

4.30–5pm Dump, change, refuel

5–7.30pm Study with breaks

7.30–9pm Eat dinner/catch up with social media/do any of the other stuff you want

You could wake up at 7am and have got a **full 9 hours sleep**. So, there **are** enough hours in the day for everything, but **only if you plan**. It's a good idea to let your friends know in advance you'll be unavailable between 5 and 7.30pm. You could even have an agreement that none of you go online between those hours, thus swerving the dreaded FOMO.

SECTION 4
TESTS AND EXAMS

So we can't avoid it any longer, all this studying is to prepare you for testing. Assessments and exams are an increasingly regular part of life at secondary school, with end of year exams taking place in the summer every year to prepare you for the big ones in years 11 and 13. And they're something we can't avoid, so we need to be able to face them without falling apart.

KEEPING CALM

Most of the panic we feel has to do ultimately with our **breathing** and **heart rate**. If you can regulate those, you'll feel at least 50% better.

BREATHING

If you find you are breathing in a fast, shallow way, bear in mind you will already have too much oxygen in your body, which can in turn make you feel light-headed and sick. Therefore, when you regulate the breath, always start by breathing out.

Breathe out for a slow count of five through your mouth . . .

and then **breathe in** for a slow count of five through your nose, taking the breaths deeply from your chest.

Repeat this three times, then see if you can breathe out for a slow count of seven and in for just five.

If you have trouble counting slowly when you are feeling panicked (which is completely understandable), try doing it to the count of a slow song in your head. (At the moment I'm using 'Shallow' by Lady Gaga and Bradley Cooper but it can be anything with a ballady-type beat).

RELAXATION

The best way I have found to control my panic is to first 'lean in' to any anxiety I feel by clenching every muscle in my body for a count of five. I clench my jaw, fists, buttocks – any part of my body which is clench-able – and then release for a count of seven, whilst breathing out. I was taught this technique by a therapist who said if you feel nervous, you should try to embrace the feeling before letting it go – a bit like a surfer does when riding a wave.

POWER POSES

Claire Eastham is author of *We're All Mad Here: A No Nonsense Guide to Living with Social Anxiety*. When she feels nervous before an event, she uses **'power posing'**.

Claire first learned about power posing from a 2012 TED talk by Amy Cuddy. In the talk, Cuddy argues that our body language governs the way we feel about ourselves. Research conducted by Cuddy and her team found that changing our stance actually impacts body chemistry.

In the study, people asked to adopt 'power poses' - standing tall with their feet apart and their shoulders back - demonstrated a measurable rise in testosterone (which makes you feel more confident) and lower levels of cortisol. In essence, it was found that the body is capable of 'tricking' the mind into being calmer.

Claire first used this technique in 2017, before going on stage to talk in front of five hundred people. This would be a daunting task for most of us, but Claire has been diagnosed with acute social anxiety, which means she is in a constant state of 'fight or flight'. She rolled her shoulders back, stood tall, held her head high and, just for added flourish, put her hands on her hips 'like Wonder Woman'. She found that her anxiety decreased, along with her desire to run away.

You can try adopting this power pose before you walk into any stressful situation, or even a presentation or an exam. If there are people watching and it makes you feel like a politician possessed by an alien in an episode of Doctor Who, then wait until you're seated at your desk. Sit tall with your back straight against the chair. Roll your shoulders back and sit straight. Place your hands firmly on the desk in front of you as if, in Claire's words, 'this desk belongs to YOU'. Take a deep breath and smile (everyone else will be too engrossed in their own business to notice or care about why you're grinning oddly).

This should encourage a flow of positive energy which will leave you in a clearer, more confident frame of mind.

FIGHT, FLIGHT OR FREEZE

As we've already explored, there's a high chance you're going to be in 'fight, flight or freeze' mode when you're heading into a stressful situation. This in turn increases the chances of you not being able to recall the information you've studied or not giving the situation your best shot.

It is, therefore, worth spending two to five minutes doing a simple **mindfulness activity** to get you out of fight or flight before you get started.

MINDFULNESS

Mindfulness is a skill, which means you can't just pull it out of the bag when you urgently need it without having practised it. If you're going to use this technique, make sure you incorporate mindfulness into your study break-up activities in Section 3. Try using an app like CALM or Headspace, which take you on guided mindfulness activities.

Once you're in the exam, or in the moment, **don't worry** about what other people are doing. Getting yourself into the right frame of mind means you are using your time more wisely and are likely to perform better than, for example, those who start furiously scribbling the minute you're told to turn over your papers.

Quick Mindfulness Activities

1. 'Anchor yourself' by concentrating on the feeling of your feet on the floor and your back against your chair. Really focus on that and nothing else whilst breathing slowly and deeply for a couple of minutes.

2. Count what you can see in the room. For example, you might count the objects on your desk, or the lines in the pattern on the floor beneath your desk.

PANIC ATTACKS

Panic attacks are an extreme manifestation of the 'fight, flight or freeze' response explained in Section 1. When we're overwhelmed with adrenaline it can cause heart palpitations, light-headedness, overheating, sweating, trembling, nausea, chest pains, shortness of breath, a sensation akin to being strangled, jelly-legs and a general feeling of being disconnected from your surroundings. Panic attacks are exactly as fun as you might imagine, having read that description.

If you're prone to anxiety, or even if you aren't, panic attacks are more likely in highly stressful situations.

I've experienced panic attacks for most of my life and have learned that the best way to manage them is to catch them in the early stages. This can be tricky, since the way an attack manifests can vary dramatically – whilst one person might start hyperventilating, another might look entirely calm from the outside whilst their brain is doing somersaults inside their skull.

If you've had panic attacks in the past, try to document how they tend to play out, in your experience. I find it's useful to plot the **stages of an attack** between one and ten. For instance, when I have a panic attack it usually goes like this:

1. I begin to feel irritable for no real reason

2. Random, irrational thoughts pop into my head, sometimes involving upsetting memories

3. Sounds seem unreasonably loud* (for example, a person talking on their phone nearby which didn't bother me five minutes ago suddenly seems deafening)

4. I have difficulty concentrating

5. My environment starts to go in and out of focus

6. Colours appear more vibrant, like I was inside an SD TV show but now it's been switched to HD*

7. My throat begins to feel tight

8. I become aware that I'm struggling to breathe

9. I hyperventilate

10. I find it difficult to stand

---

* These are both examples of my brain preparing me for 'fight or flight'. In an encounter with a predator, having magnified senses is an essential superpower. Unfortunately (or perhaps fortunately) however, school is not a tiger-filled plain.

IN MY EXPERIENCE, IF YOU CAN 'CATCH' THE PANIC ATTACK BEFORE STEP 5, IT'S MUCH EASIER TO DIAL YOURSELF BACK OUT OF ANXIETY.

Below are a couple of techniques I find useful:

1 CLENCH AND RELEASE (as described on page 127)

Think of panic like a wave. If you try to fight the wave while its cresting, then the chances are it will knock you over. But, if you 'lean in' to the feeling of panic and then ride the wave as it crashes to shore, you can bring your brain and body into alignment, thus ensuring you can regain control.

2 USE YOUR SURROUNDINGS

Challenge yourself to name five things you can see or hear in your surroundings. This is a mindfulness exercise and will help to anchor you back into the moment, rather than spiral into panic.

Traditional wisdom tells us to focus on breathing to combat a panic attack. However, the latest thinking is that this can cause yet more anxiety, since it draws our attention to the fact that we're not breathing normally. That being said, if you find breathing exercises useful and want to continue to use them, remember to ALWAYS breathe out first.

IF YOU'VE NEVER HAD A PANIC ATTACK BEFORE, OR IF YOU HAVE AND ARE AWARE THAT YOU'VE PASSED STAGE 5, IT'S PROBABLY BEST TO LET IT HAPPEN.

There is a point at which a full-on attack becomes inevitable, and if you try to fight it your body will send in yet more adrenaline (to try to fight the adrenaline – which is a fundamental human design flaw akin to the inside of your mouth swelling up when you bite it) and this will make the eventual attack even worse. Again, try to think of your anxiety as a wave – lean into it and let it happen.

If the panic attack happens **whilst you're in class**, put your hand up, explain what has happened to a teacher (if you're able) and ask if you can pop out for two minutes of fresh air. When you're outdoors, do some stretches to try to minimize the adrenaline in your system. **Flop forward** so your fingertips touch your toes and breathe deeply. Do this a few times and, when you walk back into class, visualize **closing the door** on your anxiety and leaving it outside.

If you have a panic attack **outside of class**, remember that they use up a lot of energy and can leave you feeling exhausted – have a quick nap or lie-down afterwards, if you can, (twenty minutes is ideal) and/or a snack. If you think a panic attack is likely, carry something like raw nuts and dried fruit or an energy ball with you to give you a boost afterwards.

WHAT TO DO IF YOU SEE SOMEONE HAVING A PANIC ATTACK

- Without touching them (unless they ask you to) try to manoeuvre them to a place where they can either sit down or have their back against a wall (so if they faint they have something to support their fall).

- Reassure them that you will stay with them until the attack is over and that they are safe.

- Ask them to tell you five things they can see or hear (see technique 2 on page 133) until their breathing returns to normal.

- When the attack is over, ask them what they need, for example some people like to be taken away from any crowds, others like to have people around them.

- Try to resist the urge to interrogate them about what caused it – they might not know or want to talk about it. But let them know you're there if they do want to talk.

For more information on panic and anxiety, have a look at the organizations listed at the back of this book.

EXAM SEASON is always celebrated within the media by celebrities gleefully tweeting or giving interviews about how they left school with no qualifications whatsoever and now they're a hugely successful multi-gazillionaire. I *think* I understand why. It's to **comfort** those who might not have done as well as they'd hoped. Yet I always think it's kinda **disrespectful** to all the people who've worked their bee-hinds off to be told exams 'don't matter'.

It's also dishonest.

Tests and exams *do* matter.

Perhaps they shouldn't, but until the revolution comes they're the way students are assessed and what allows them to go on to the next stage of their education/life. True, an incredibly lucky **0.00001% of the population** might be plucked from obscurity and have a no. 1 hit record or be given their own TV show, but they're not really relevant to most people's experience.

Having said all that, tests and exams **don't** matter as much as, say, being a decent person. If you don't tend to perform well under exam conditions, or unavoidable circumstances mean you aren't able to give your best, you shouldn't write yourself off. **There are other ways to succeed in life.**

Ultimately, everyone should just **do their best** and then give themselves massive props because their best is, by definition, **all they can do.**

That means being **realistic** about what tests and exams are – **a means to an end**. They aren't measuring your worth as a person or indeed anything more significant than your ability to reproduce the things you've learnt under timed conditions.

With that in mind, create two lists representing what tests and exams do and do not mean, to you. That way, as they get closer and closer you can refer back to them to remind yourself they are **quite** important (but not *that* important). I've added an example to get you started . . .

TESTS AND EXAMS ARE:
A way for me to get to the next stage

TESTS AND EXAMS ARE NOT:
Measuring my value as a person

REMEMBERING YOUR VALUE

Shahroo Izadi, author of the bestselling *The Kindness Method*, says that in order to understand our own behaviours we have to first look at how our beliefs and habits serve us (or once did). For example, looking back at Section 2, we see that if you're an epic procrastinator then everyone around you might assume you're just lazy. Yet we know procrastination can be sparked by a fear of failure and therefore might be your mind's way of actually protecting you from something you're frightened of. You'd have to know yourself pretty well to arrive at that conclusion and be in a position to make meaningful change.

Shahroo advises keeping a log of your achievements via a map. Write 'My Strengths and Achievements' in the centre of a piece of paper and circle it. Then draw branches listing anything that happens throughout the study period that gives you a sense of satisfaction, whether that's finally wrapping your head around a complex piece of algebra or something simple like *'it was sunny and I really wanted to go to the park with my friends but I stuck to my revision plan'*.

You should also note down timeless qualities you like about yourself (for example, *'I am funny'* or *'I am kind'*) or previous examples of times you have felt proud of yourself (*'I raised money for charity'* or *'I helped my mum when she was sick'*). Keep the map visible while revising.

On the morning of your test or exam, take a few minutes to look at your map. Remind yourself that you are capable of learning, progress and achievement. Assure yourself also that, even if for some reason the exam doesn't go to plan, there are so many qualities on your map which don't depend on grades – they'll all still be there once the exam is over.

I am kind

I raised money for
charity

My strengths and achievements

I am funny

I helped Mum
when she was sick

EXAM DAY

WHAT *NOT* TO DO

As previously alluded to, there was one exam I failed spectacularly during my academic career. It was my 'S' level English (which is between an A level and degree) and was taught by a genius eccentric called Dr Cochran – a Byron and Tarantino fanatic and with the best eyebrows I've ever seen on a human. Let the record state that my failure was in no way a reflection of his ability.

What happened was this: **I'd written down the time of the exam wrong.** I thought it was in the afternoon, it was actually in the morning. I was shaken awake by my mum at approx. 9.15am, when my concerned teacher had rung our house phone (yes, it was the olden days) to ask why I hadn't shown.

I panicked utterly and completely. I castigated myself approximately 200,000 times. I spent more time than I technically had wishing I had done physics so I might be able to work out how to build a time machine and go back and change the mistake.

I threw on some clothes, Mum was already there in her car with the engine running and she threw a box of strawberries and blueberries at me to eat as we sped to my school on one wheel because 'you can't do an exam on an empty stomach' (very true, Mum).

I arrived panicked, sweaty, smelly, remorseful and nauseous. As a result, I didn't read the instructions properly and only answered two essay questions rather than the required three.

WHAT YOU SHOULD DO

You should try, if at all possible, to get a good night's sleep the night before. Set **two alarms** and ask a member of your family to check you're awake ten minutes after. That way, you won't wake up every half an hour drenched in sweat, having had a recurring nightmare where you **sleep through** your exam.

If your exam is in the morning, concentrate on getting yourself physically and mentally prepared, rather than trying to cram in **extra revision** at the last minute. If your exam is in the afternoon, you can take the morning to do some extra revision, but remember this **isn't** the time to be learning new concepts. Instead, go back over your mind maps or summary sheets to refresh your memory on what you have already learned.

HERE ARE SOME TIPS FOR KEEPING YOURSELF CALM AND FOCUSED.

BREAKFAST

Even if you feel sick with nerves, try to eat a little something so your stomach doesn't begin growling distractingly mid-exam. Ideally, you'll want to eat something filling but not so heavy as to make you feel sluggish. A few ideas are:

PORRIDGE

Porridge is one of the cheapest, quickest and most nutritious things you can eat. Just fill a mug about halfway with porridge oats, then add to a pan with a full mug of any type of milk you fancy (I prefer soya, because it adds a natural sweetness). Gently heat the porridge, stirring every so often and adding more milk depending on your favoured consistency. When the porridge looks creamy and . . . well . . . like porridge, it's ready to eat. Add banana, berries, honey, seeds or dried fruit for extra flavour.

SCRAMBLED EGGS AND AVOCADO ON TOAST

This will keep you full for AGES, particularly if you use whole-wheat bread.

YOGURT, BERRIES AND GRANOLA/SEEDS

This is what I eat when I can't really be bothered with breakfast. It's quick and delicious, which means I pretty much always want to eat it, even when I feel a bit sick. I use Greek yogurt because it has a nice, neutral flavour and has a good, thick consistency, then add blueberries, granola and sunflower seeds.

CAFFEINE

You might be tempted to down 17 cups of coffee or a tonne of energy drink before your exam to make you hyper-awake, but this is a plan **doomed to failure**. It means you'll crash a few hours later (probably mid-exam) and also guarantees you'll need a wee at an inappropriate moment.

If you're used to coffee, drink **one cup** as early as possible after waking to get your system going, if your exam's in the morning. If it's in the afternoon, drink your cup of coffee between one and two hours beforehand. There's some evidence to show green tea can improve alertness but, again, restrict it to one cup (also, it is in my opinion **vile**, so hold your nose whilst drinking).

IF YOU STRUGGLE TO FEEL ALERT IN THE MORNINGS, TRY GOING FOR A TEN-MINUTE BRISK WALK OR HAVING A COOL SHOWER TO WAKE YOURSELF UP.

STAYING COOL

WHY-OH-WHY DO EXAMS HAVE TO HAPPEN IN SUMMER?

NO ONE PERFORMS AT THEIR BEST WHEN THEY ARE A SWEATY MESS

(FACT).

It seems so stupid to me that the time of year when even your most entertaining teacher struggles to hold your attention – because the combination of soaring temperatures and the smell of freshly cut grass produce the overwhelming desire to sleep in a field – is when they choose to have the examination period.

Anyway, perhaps more importantly, according to the charity 'No Panic' (details at the back of this book), hot weather can produce symptoms similar to those of **anxiety** (shortness of breath, feeling irritable and sweaty), particularly if the pollen count is high.

If your exam happens to be on a day like this, try the following:

- If you **don't** have to wear your uniform, keep your clothing loose and, if possible, made of breathable fibres (like cotton).

- Invest in a hand-held **fan.** You probably won't be allowed to take it into the exam room with you, but you can at least use it to keep yourself cool until you cross the threshold.

- Fill a **squirty bottle** with cold water and spray over your face keeping it away from your eyes (add a few drops of ylang ylang or lavender essential oil to keep you calm, or cedarwood, peppermint or rosemary for a 'focusing' effect).

- Before the exam, go to the loo and run your wrists under the **cold tap** of the sink for about 90 seconds on each side. Apparently, this cools the entire blood stream (you 'catch' the blood as it circulates around your body, since your wrists are where it is closest to the surface).

PLANNING

IF YOU HAVE MORE THAN ONE EXAM IN A DAY

Having two or more exams in one day is really bad luck. If this happens to you: sorry. **That sucks.**

Planning is everything in these circumstances, so make sure you have a strategy in place which will allow you to 'shake off' the first exam and prepare yourself for the next. Let's say you have a one-hour break, you may wish to divide it up like this:

First 20 minutes – Go for a walk/get some fresh air and release the adrenaline built up in your system as a result of the exam you have just had.

Second 20 minutes – Refresh and refuel – if you can, have a quick wash or shower. Have a snack with slow-release energy to prepare you for the next exam.

Last 20 minutes – Look over a few of your mind maps or revision cards for the forthcoming exam, or practise your knowledge with a friend, to get yourself into the right headspace.

Make sure when you're packing your bag the previous evening you take into account what you'll need for break period (e.g. revision notes, water, snacks, a change of T-shirt to help you feel 'fresh').

PLANNING IN THE EXAM ITSELF

You know how long you have to do the exam and the paper will tell you how many questions you have to answer (sometimes you have to do them all, sometimes you can pick and choose from each section). **Before you begin, designate time to each question.**

> For example, if you have to do two essays and four shorter questions and have two and a half hours, you can dedicate **ten minutes** to planning/mindfulness, **50 minutes** to each essay question and **ten minutes** to each shorter question.

Be disciplined, even if you haven't finished the question you're on. If the time is up, move on to the next one. Because of the (slightly daft, in my opinion) way exams are marked, you get awarded points for each correct observation you make in an essay, as opposed to being rewarded for writing it well and finishing it beautifully.

So, you'll achieve a higher grade by answering all the questions, even if you don't finish them, than if you spent all your time on one (even if you answer that one more brilliantly than Einstein himself could ever have dreamed).

If you have time at the end you can always go back to any unfinished parts.

KEEP AN EYE ON MARKS

The exam paper will state **how many marks** can be awarded for each question. Therefore, even if you know lots about a topic, make sure you only spend the amount of time appropriate to the total amount of marks you can be awarded.

RECREATE YOUR MIND MAPS

When revising, you might have used **imagery** to help 'lock in' the information you were studying. See what happens if you start recreating some of those pictures by **doodling** at the top of your exam paper. With any luck, you'll find your revision comes flooding back to you.

DO THE EASIEST QUESTIONS FIRST

Remember, you don't have to do the questions **in the order they are listed** on the exam paper (just make sure you indicate **clearly** which question you are answering in the margin). If there is a question that you feel very confident answering, **do that first** to get your intellectual juices flowing. Answering easier questions first also ensures you are scooping up the maximum marks in the allocated time.

PLAN YOUR ESSAYS

You're never going to produce the greatest essay you're capable of under exam conditions. Fortunately, the examiner isn't looking for how well you articulate yourself, merely that you have **understood** the point you're making/recalled key information and, in the case of English, can **quote directly** from the text.

Your essay should have an **introduction, middle part and conclusion**. Plan your middle part and lay out the key points you want to make in it on your paper, before beginning the essay. That way, even if you don't get the chance to complete the essay, the examiner can see what you would have said if you'd had the time and may choose to award you **extra points.**

SHOW YOUR WORKINGS

For longer maths or science questions, it's really important to show **how you arrived at the answers** you have. That way, if you miscalculate the examiner can see you were at least using the **correct methodology**, which is a large part of how you are graded.

DON'T

- **Look at anyone else.** You'll get a fit of the giggles or, worse still, you'll be accused of cheating.
- **Leave the exam** within the first 20 minutes. If you find yourself thinking 'this is too hard!' that's your amygdala talking. Do your mindfulness activity and try again.
- **Look** at the exam questions or start writing **before** the invigilator instructs you to do so.
- **Forget** that however laid-back/amusing the invigilating teacher is, circumstances dictate that they must become an aloof, scary person for the duration of the exam.

DO

- Make sure you arrive about 20 minutes **before** the exam is due to begin.
- **Cross through your rough notes** (but do so in such a way as they are still legible to the examiner – just put one long, diagonal line through them).
- Use **black ink** only.
- **Raise your hand** to attract the attention of the invigilator if you need the loo or feel ill.

AND FINALLY...

REMEMBER, YOU GOT THIS. MILLIONS OF PEOPLE JUST LIKE YOU HAVE TAKEN EXAMS AND SURVIVED.

THE AFTERMATH

IF AT ALL POSSIBLE, you should **disregard** anything your classmates say to you either directly before the exam or straight after it. The reason for this is that you are probably all off your noggins on nervous energy and the consequent chemical changes that will induce.

I learned this from watching my husband, who is in a rock band, perform. Before he goes on stage it's like he is cocooned in cotton wool. He has no concept of what I'm saying to him and will just bleat out his thoughts at random, regardless of what I've just said. After the performance he's **high as a kite** on relief and euphoria and asks me about 47,000 times if he 'did alright'. In neither state is he remotely rational and he often doesn't remember the conversations we've had.

Exams are a performance of sorts and it's likely you'll go through the same stages of tunnel-visioned anticipation and light-headed relief. The chances are you won't consider even for a moment how anything you say or do might impact the people around you, which goes some way to explaining the things other people will say to you as soon as you're allowed to talk, post-exam. Things like:

> **How do you think you did?**

> **Did you see the question on the back of the last page?**

> **What did you get for question 3a?**

They're framed as **questions** directed at you, but the person asking them is not really listening to your replies. This conversation is **all about them** – it's their attempt to reassure themselves that they 'did alright'. Even the cleverest person in your class will feel this urge – they aren't showing off (however much it might sound as though they are) - they're **self-soothing** after a minor traumatic experience.

These discussions need to happen, but you're all just **babbling nonsense**. Too much time spent analyzing an exam you've already taken achieves precisely nothing –

YOU CAN'T CHANGE THE PAST.

So, make a pact with your friends that you'll spend a finite amount of time dwelling. Use this promise card:

I HEREBY PROMISE

TO SPEND A MAXIMUM OF _____ MINUTES
THINKING ABOUT/DISCUSSING/SEARCHING
ON SOCIAL MEDIA MY EXAM PAPER
AFTER IT HAS HAPPENED.

Keep a **red card** in your bag. When time's up, flash the red card to signal that you should change the subject. Ideally, you should have planned in advance what you're going to do or talk about next.

You could, for example, all agree ahead of the exam to watch an episode of something on Netflix that's easy to enthusiastically dissect and switch to discussing that.

You'll also need to physically **'shake off'** the chemical impact of the exam. The previous section will help you minimize the fight, flight or freeze mechanism during the exam itself, but the experience will still have had a lasting effect on your body's chemical balance. As with your revision break-up activities, your goal should be to create **endorphins**. You'll probably be too buzzy to meditate, so try going for a walk or punching a punch bag or pillow.

You could also try watching some **stand-up** on YouTube (laughter releases endorphins).

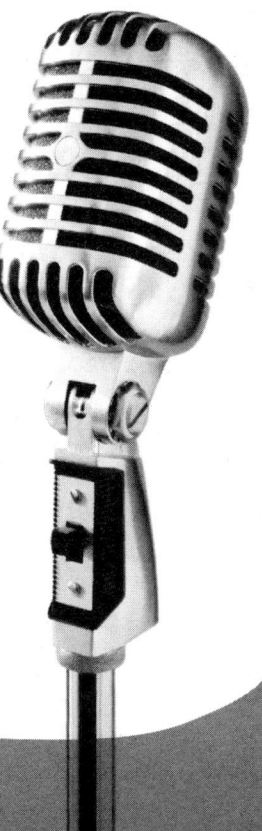

RESULTS DAY

Inevitably, writing this book has brought back a lot of memories linked to **my own experience of exams**. In particular it's made me think about my A levels, because that's the time when I studied the hardest, revised the most diligently, had the best comparative mental health (when I took my GCSEs I was in recovery from anorexia and at university I had bulimia).

As a result of all of these things, I got the best grades.

I remember A level results day vividly. I remember I'd been out the night before with my friend Lucy-the-Spurs-Fan and we'd drunk several bottles of Smirnoff Ice (a type of alcopop that tasted of sweet lemonade) in her local pub. I remember staying at her parents' house and the next morning putting on my pre-planned 'results day' outfit of white cut-off jeans and a mint green 'rib top' (so-called because it was made of ribbed cotton)[*]. I remember my mum came to pick us up and drive us to school to collect our results (this was before you could have them emailed) and that Ronan Keating's 'You Say it Best When You Say Nothing at All' from the movie *Notting Hill* was playing on the radio (to this day that song makes me feel a bit sick at the memory of pre-results nerves combined with mild hangover).

When we arrived at school, there were already some students from my year on the steps that led up to the entrance hall with ripped envelopes in their hands. I looked at one of them and

---

[*] It was the 90s and therefore no one is allowed to judge me for my fashion choices.

smiled. She immediately put her arm around a girl standing next to her and shouted 'WE'RE NOT TELLING ANYONE WHAT WE GOT', in response to a question I hadn't even asked. My heart was pounding so hard I could hear my pulse in my ears, like the tide going in and out. My English teacher came up and handed me my envelope, smiled conspiratorially and said 'well done' which made me think:

a) everything was going to be okay and

b) it was a bit unfair that she knew what I'd got before I did.

I remember for some reason wanting to prolong the moment before I opened my envelope. It was a sort of 'Schrödinger's Cat'-type impulse, I was practising in my mind what it would feel like to have passed **and** failed during a beat in time when either was a possibility. When I eventually saw the three As my overwhelming feelings were relief and concern that I was dreaming. I gave myself a pinch just to check.

A really annoying girl in my year came right up to me and stuck her face in mine so our noses were almost touching. **'WHAT DID YOU GET?'** she demanded. I understood, now, why the people on the steps were so defensive. I was aware I didn't want to sound like I was too pleased, in case she thought I was showing off. I almost whispered my reply, to which she said **'YOU KNEW YOU'D DO WELL'**, like it was an accusation.

A reporter from the local newspaper was hovering with a camera and our (extremely cool, David Bowie-lookalike) headteacher grabbed me by the elbow and instructed me to join the group of students being interviewed. 'How do you feel?' the reporter asked. I replied,

'WELL, WHEN I WOKE UP I WAS HAVING A FAT DAY SO I KNEW I'D DO WELL BECAUSE YOU WOULDN'T HAVE TWO THINGS GO WRONG IN ONE DAY.'

I HAVE LITERALLY NO IDEA WHAT POSSESSED ME TO SAY THAT.

I'd never used the term 'fat day' before in my whole entire life (and haven't since). Also, OF COURSE two things can go wrong in one day. I think I thought I was being funny. Clearly, I wasn't. I was being a tool.

The moral of this memory is that, just like after exams, people say and do really strange things on results day. The combination of adrenaline, exhilaration for some and crushing disappointment for others means a general group state of super-heightened emotion. It's little surprise really. So much hinges on that day. It's almost like your whole life, up until then, has been pointing at it. It's the bittersweet mix of celebration and sadness at the end of an era, coupled with the inevitable follow-up thought of 'what next'? It's also a judgement, handed down from on high, your entire education reduced to a single letter of the alphabet.

It's not true that you can sum up a person's value, intelligence or experience in a grade, of course, but it doesn't feel like that at the time.

People behave completely out of character on results day, saying things they don't mean, and will spend a lifetime furtively kicking their duvet in the wee small hours as they try to banish it from their 'embarrassing incidents which torture us in the night' memory banks.

You should disregard anything anyone says to you on this day and try to forgive yourself for your responses, too.

ADULT RESPONSES

Be aware that adults aren't immune from saying dumb stuff. There are some tips for conflict resolution in the final section of this book but, just to prepare you for what you might hear, I asked my Twitter following what were the worst things adults had said to them post-exam (interestingly, there was no shortage of replies from people in their 30s, 40s and beyond – they all remembered vividly). Here are some of them:

> **'And are YOU pleased with that?'**
> (in a sneering sort of way)

> (After the results of a test I got 99.5% on)
> **'What happened to the other .5%?'**

> **'Why did you only get a B?'**

'That paper should have been easy, for you.'

(On hearing that I'd got mostly Bs and Cs in my GCSEs) 'Oh well, never mind.'

'Not everyone is academic, I suppose.'

All of the people on the receiving end of these comments went on to lead happy and successful lives.

SECTION 5
THE NEXT CHAPTER

SCHOOL is a series of transitions. Year 7 is all about getting settled in a new environment – a bigger school, more subjects, more lessons, more teachers and more homework, not to mention having to make new friends. Then you gradually specialize as you approach year 11 and GCSEs, before yet making more decisions about what to study next. By year 13 it's making decisions about uni, gap years or apprenticeships. It can feel really overwhelming.

If you're struggling to come to any sort of decision about the next chapter, seek advice from a wide range of sources and remember that all anyone can ever offer you is the benefit of their perspective. However extensive this is, it doesn't give them the right to tell you how you should live your life.

It might very well be that the thing you end up doing for a living is a job you aren't currently aware of, or that hasn't

been invented, yet. When I was at school, given as I was to trouncing everyone in debating competitions, I was constantly being told I should be a lawyer. I understood why people said this. I have a brain that makes connections between seemingly unrelated things (which is handy if you're attempting to argue that your client's libel case is actually most relevant to a precedent set by a 1914 dispute between farmers over who owned a sheep which had inexplicably decided to leap over a hedge).

However, some gut instinct stopped me from studying law at uni and when I tried training as a paralegal in my early twenties **I despised everything about it**. For me, law was less what you see on TV (glamorous people defending wrongly accused victims by making eloquent speeches in shiny court rooms) and more endless photocopying whilst having life mansplained to you.

I didn't know at sixteen I'd end up being an activist and author because I didn't know anyone back then who did that. I wasn't even aware it was a thing. My degree in English hasn't helped in the classic sense, in that qualifications aren't really a 'thing' in my line of work, but having a certain level of education has, I believe, immeasurably enhanced the experience of living in my brain. That's before you factor in the experiences I had and the friends I made at university, as well as how handy having a basic knowledge of law is when you're lobbying businesses and governments as a campaigner. **Given my time again, I'd make exactly the same decisions.**

This is all a very convoluted way of saying two things:

1   People's lives are very rarely linear, but every false start teaches you something valuable (even if that's finding out what you don't want to do).

2   Before you get to the BIG exams (GCSEs and A levels) you're never properly thinking about life after exams, so the chances are the day you do your last exam you'll feel a mild sensation of existential despair. This chapter is designed to help you harness that feeling and channel it into something useful and productive.

YEAR 8 TO 9

I've been visiting schools for a really long time now and it always seems to be like year 9 is the time *everything* happens. Usually, at least a couple of people in the year come out as LGBTQ. Lots of people make their first forays into romantic relationships. Many people start their periods and voices start to break.

> year 9 is the time *everything* happens

I also notice that year 9 groups tend to start segregating themselves by gender, most of the boys sit on one side of the room and most of the girls on the other. The audiences I speak to also become a bit more self-conscious and sometimes reluctant to stick their hands up and ask or answer a question.

I suppose this is all a very long-winded way of saying: **HORMONES**. (Also, that if you have noticed these things happening around you it's all totally normal).

I think it's this context which makes year 9 seem like such a big change, rather than it marking a huge academic leap. You might have seen that some schools start preparing their pupils for GSCEs now in year 9 (rather than in year 10, as traditional) but don't worry: that just means they start specializing and reducing the number of subjects each pupil studies, not that the work becomes harder, earlier.

I spoke to Cathy Walker, Head of Education Development at the Girls Day School Trust. She described being in year 9 as a bit like being 'the middle child' in a family – you're not the babies of the school like you are in years 7 and 8, but you're not in charge like the year 10s and 11s are. She also said year 9 was a really good opportunity to 'scaffold your learning' – to build good habits which will serve you well in the years to come. It's a time when you can make mistakes (which are actually crucial to the learning process and not a sign of failure) and think about *how* you learn, rather than just *what* you're learning. Cathy collated some tips from members of staff across GDST schools on how to navigate the transition from years 8 to 9.

Here is a summary of what they said:

1. Think about your goals – what do you want to achieve, by when and why? This could be career aspirations, next steps e.g. A Levels or you might simply enjoy learning for learning's sake. You could talk to your form tutor or your school's career's advisor about this to help you form a vision of what your future could look like.

2. Making wise choices for GCSE option subjects involves making sure you have a mixture of things you love and are passionate about and those things which will support your goals.

3. As you go through your education, there will be more and more independent learning, so it's always worth dedicating time to practising this and noticing what

works and what doesn't, for you – go back to the sections on motivation and time management for some practical tips.

4. You'll start to do more extended writing around this time so develop good techniques such as planning answers before you start writing and always including an introduction and conclusion.

5. Act on feedback – teachers spend a lot of time marking pupils' work and offering suggestions to improve. If you didn't do as well as you'd hoped, see it as an opportunity to grow and do better next time.

This is also a good year to build the foundations which will support your wellbeing as you move on to GCSEs and beyond. Knowing how much sleep you need and what contributes to you getting a good quality night's kip, for example. Or making sure you have subjects outside of school you're curious and passionate about by reading non-curriculum books, magazines or listening to podcasts. These are skills which will serve you throughout the rest of your life so it's a good investment of your time to nail them now.

GCSE TO A LEVEL

Academically, GCSE to A level is the **biggest leap** you will make. Don't let that worry you, though: in my experience that just means everything's about to get a whole lot more interesting. You've significantly streamlined the amount of subjects you're studying and hopefully boiled them down to the ones that genuinely fascinate you the most.

The biggest difference between A levels and the school experience which precedes them is the amount of independent study you're expected to do. You'll have 'free periods', during which it is expected you'll work. This requires a lot of self-discipline (especially when there's always a group in your year who will decide to sunbathe/go to the nearest pub/Starbucks).

I struggle with self-discipline. I love being busy, but perform best when I have a sense of urgency because the project is time-sensitive. If you are like me, try setting yourself 'mini deadlines' and rope in a teacher, friend or parent to make sure you stick to them. For example, if you have an essay of 1,000 words due in a week, divide that into 250 words per day and tell another person you'll email it to them section by section. It doesn't matter whether they read it or not, simply that you have made a promise to another person and they can nudge you if you're sliding.

The pace at which you'll work will change at A level, so if you've been given a set reading list for the summer holidays, **make sure you actually read them.**

> # IT'S MUCH HARDER TO WING IT AT THIS LEVEL.

I'm not suggesting that you finish your last GCSE and immediately go home and bury yourself in a mountain of A level text books, just that the time for celebration/letting loose should be **finite**. Give yourself a proportion (say, two weeks) of the six-week holiday to party/holiday and generally let off steam and the rest to prepare for the next phase and slowly, gently, get yourself back into the studying mindset.

GCSE TO COLLEGE

Colleges are brilliant. I went to the sixth form of the school I attended for five years to do my A Levels, so in terms of a change in culture the only difference was that we had a common room and didn't have to wear our schools' beyond-hideous sludge-brown uniform any more (I burned mine in a ceremonial gesture in my back garden after finishing year 11).

Colleges are a different thing altogether – they feel totally different from school. You're treated and spoken to like a proper adult and are usually allowed to have bright pink hair and 17 studs in each ear, should you wish.

Be aware that there will be an unsettling period where you try to work out how you fit into this new environment. At school, everyone acquires a **reputation** as something – the class clown, the introvert, the swot, the sporty one – really quickly. Despite the fact that these labels are very often not based in reality, but are more a reflection of everyone's desire to 'get the measure' of one another, once you are branded as such it's incredibly hard to shake off that identity. At college, those labels won't apply any more. It's an opportunity to reinvent yourself, but that can also be a confusing and time-consuming process when you also have work to do.

Try not to overthink it. College exposes you to a wider range of people, which means an opportunity to sit back, observe and take inspiration. Ultimately, all our personalities are composed of elements borrowed from other people's and everyone we interact with in a meaningful way leaves a kind of footprint. See this as an opportunity to experiment and evolve.

The advice above about independent study also applies to college. You'll be micromanaged a lot less than at school, which will probably initially be both a relief and a bit scary.

CLOTHES

A quick note here for anyone entering a phase of their life where they no longer have to wear a uniform every day: for about three days, this will be the best thing that has ever happened to you. After that, it will be a giant pain.

Deciding what to wear in the morning, particularly during a period of your life where you're experimenting with identity, takes forever. It's therefore best to plan in advance lest ye be perpetually late for everything.

When I was in sixth form my identity was the 'I don't care about being fashionable or glamorous because I am terribly clever and therefore those things are beneath me' person. I therefore went to Marks & Spencer and bought five identical pairs of boot-leg trousers in navy and black and simply alternated them with various slouchy jumpers and shirts. I'm not saying this is for everyone, but it did give me more time to actually do my A levels.

A LEVEL TO UNI

Whilst the transition from A level to degree is academically less steep than GCSE to A level, the change in your lifestyle will be sudden and dramatic.

THIS MIGHT EXPLAIN WHY THE MOVE TO UNIVERSITY IS CONSISTENTLY CITED BY THE PEOPLE I TALK TO AS THE TIME THEY REALLY BEGAN TO STRUGGLE WITH THEIR EMOTIONAL AND MENTAL HEALTH.

Don't let this stress you unduly. For most people, university is the first time they have lived away from their family home and so a certain amount of turmoil, homesickness and feelings of uncertainty are inevitable. The key is to try to tune in to how exciting this period of your life is and minimize any unnecessary distress.

As already mentioned, everyone has an invisible safety net beneath them. It's composed of the people in their network, the activities they do to keep themselves sane and the procedures or techniques which are in place to help them if they are visibly struggling. The first step in anticipating the impact that moving to university might have on you is to identify what your safety net looks like now and which parts are going to shift when you leave home.

Try completing the following sentences, as a start:

> When I have a friendship issue I talk to . . .
>
> When I have a health issue I talk to . . .
>
> When I have an academic worry I talk to . . .

However close you are to these people currently, don't assume they will be able to play the same role in your life when you get to university. We all make promises about being 'BFFs Forever' to our sixth form or college squad, but however well-intentioned and heartfelt our vows, the chances are life will get in the way. This is actually a good thing – it indicates you are properly living it.

When you get to uni, you're going to have to assemble a different cast. Over time you'll make friends you can confide in, but unless it so-happens that you and your closest mate are going to the same uni, this will take a while. Identify as early as possible what support is available so you know who to go to in the event you need support with any of the above.

FRESHERS WEEK (the week before the university term begins in earnest where first years have the opportunity to settle in) is always a good opportunity to do this. Your **student**

union will be advertising the services they have available and can usually support you with everything from housing difficulties to mental health. There'll also be representatives from various societies leaping on you enthusiastically and chewing your ear off until you relent and agree to give them your email address. It's worth going along to **at least a couple** of their meetings – it's a great (and usually free, or at least very cheap) way to meet people with similar interests.

Remember that however like a **fish-out-of-water** you feel, everyone is **in the same boat** (mixed metaphors, there). If you're living in halls, wedge your door open whenever you're in your room for the first couple of weeks. This will encourage people to pop in for a chat whenever they're passing. If you're shy, try jotting down a few conversation starters you can defer to in the event you encounter an awkward conversational silence. Things like:

> What course are you doing? What made you pick that?

> Where are you from? What's it like there?

> What made you pick this university?

> Are you going to any events this week?

Look back to Section 2 where you listed the activities which are keeping you sane. Despite the gear-shift in your lifestyle, you're still going to need these, or the nearest equivalents, at university. If you're going to a city university, spend some time doing research as to what's available in the area – many gyms, sports clubs, theatres, etc. offer student discounts, too.

> **BEAR IN MIND THAT AT UNIVERSITY IT'S MUCH EASIER TO 'FLY UNDER THE RADAR' IF YOU'RE STRUGGLING.**

Schools and colleges are a bit of a goldfish bowl, by comparison – their own little micro-communities.

Everyone knows everyone at school and if, for example, you're absent from a class a chain of consequence will be set in action which will probably result in your parents finding out. Whilst you'll still have small tutorials and seminars at uni, lectures tend to contain hundreds of students, so if you're missing, the chances are **no one will notice**.

> **THIS MEANS, WHEN IT COMES TO YOUR HEALTH AND WELLBEING, YOU HAVE TO BE MUCH MORE PROACTIVE.**

Over the summer, practise asking yourself daily to **rate your mood**. You can even keep a journal documenting how much sleep you got, what you ate and how much activity you did* and then rate your overall mood from 1-13.

---

* If you have had or are currently experiencing an eating disorder it is best to avoid documenting these as it could lead to obsessive thoughts and behaviours. Try just rating your mood each day instead.

You can then track how certain patterns of behaviour are affecting you mentally and by the time you go to university you should know what your basic requirements are for maintaining brain fitness:

> I need .... hours sleep
>
> These foods make me feel well
>
> ....
>
> I need to exercise ...... times per ....

Then ask yourself how you're going to ensure you can **continue** these behaviours at uni.

Most people drink a lot more and a hefty proportion experiment with drugs at university. Obviously I'm not advocating this, especially if you have a mental health issue (there's a lot of evidence to show excess alcohol and drugs can make your mental health worse) but I also can't stop you. If you choose to do this, know that **for every high there is a low**. The euphoria you feel whilst drunk or on drugs is just borrowing from tomorrow's stores of happiness. That isn't to say you shouldn't party, just that you should be prepared for the downs that follow the highs and put provision in place for taking extra care of yourself.

Finally, make sure you **register with a doctor** wherever you're at university, whether you're currently experiencing any health issues or not.

GAP YEAR

Whether you're working, travelling or doing a little bit of both, it's difficult to put any kind of structure or routine into a gap year. Having said that, it's worth looking at the exercise for uni students opposite and jotting down the components of your current safety net, doing some internet research and working out how you can incorporate as many aspects as possible into your adventures, in advance.

GOING INTO THE WORKPLACE/ APPRENTICESHIP

Places of work obviously vary enormously from one another, but there is one thing every newbie has in common and that is feeling like a complete tit for at least two weeks. There will be a lot of twiddling your thumbs, bothering people by asking 'is there anything I can do to help you?' and being asked to do incredibly boring and menial things like filing and making everyone tea. This is both normal and unavoidable.

The best thing you can do is use this time to create your wellness safety net/ work-life balance. Go back and read the advice for university students on page 175 about identifying the people and activities that keep you sane and building them into your new life – it's all relevant to you.

Here are some work-specific mental health strategies:

FIRSTLY AND MOST IMPORTANTLY... TAKE YOUR LUNCH BREAK

I don't care if **everyone else** in the office eats a sandwich at their desk – 'al desko' – I thank you! – we know from the previous chapters that they are damaging both their wellbeing and their afternoon productivity. It'll also become an expectation if you set a precedent early for working through your breaks.

FIND A MENTOR/CHAMPION

There should be someone at work who is in your corner and can offer you advice. It might be that you have a couple of these champions – someone who either does or once did your job and another person with whom you have something else in common. For example, if you are black, Asian or mixed race and in a minority you might want to find someone with the same heritage as you to act as your mentor. **Identify people who can give you useful information and ask if you can go for coffee.** Everyone loves feeling like they're imparting their wisdom to a grateful recipient. Also coffee.

DON'T OVER-PROMISE

There's a fine line between 'showing initiative' and signalling that you're a **pushover** who will do everyone else's work while they take the credit. It'll take a while for you to settle into a pace of work and know what you can realistically achieve in a day. Until that time, try to avoid being over-enthusiastic and taking on too much. Three Magic Words: **'I don't know'.**

DON'T GET EMBROILED IN OFFICE POLITICS

As a general rule, you should **be polite to everyone** you work with. However, there are certain stock characters you will almost certainly encounter wherever you work and who should be given a wide berth (still be polite to them, just avoid getting hoovered into their toxic web):

The office gossip – This person will invite you out for a drink early doors, during which time they will quiz you relentlessly about every aspect of your life story in between dishing dirt on their colleagues. Avoid giving them any information they can use at a later date to discredit you.

The militant 'we hate the boss' person – human energy-drainer, this person does nothing but moan. Their chair isn't comfortable enough, they are having to do a task which doesn't fit strictly within their job spec, the toilet paper in the loos isn't their preferred brand – they can always find some source of dissatisfaction and will usually imply strongly that whatever it is CONTRAVENES their WORKERS' RIGHTS. They're an eternal pessimist and if you spend too much time in their company it will rub off on you.

The 'gang member' - this person has beef with one or more other members of the work force and wants you to side with them. They'll take you under their wing, encourage you not to communicate with whoever it is they're beefing with and generally behave like something out of an American prison movie. Much like an American prison movie, the relationship rarely ends well.

IF YOU CAN'T DECIDE WHAT TO DO NEXT

If you haven't yet decided what your next chapter will be, or you've made a decision and think it might be the wrong one, it can be **incredibly difficult** to arrive at any meaningful conclusions. It's why I like to-do lists – they break everything up into bite-sized chunks so I don't have to think about the bigger picture, get completely overwhelmed and end up paralysed with contemplations of the enormity of it all.

I spoke to Dr Alan Barnard (remember him from page 38?) who said all decisions broadly fall into two categories:

> **1: DO I WANT TO DO MORE OR LESS OF SOMETHING?**

> **2: IDENTIFYING THE BEST OPTION WE HAVE.**

In order to take either type of decision, you need to first work out what your goal is. **For many people, this is the trickiest thing.** If you're struggling, try framing your goal as achieving a motivation, as outlined in Section 3, rather than a tangible job title or qualification. So your goal might be something like 'I want to make a difference', 'I want my independence' or 'I want to help others'. Write your goal at the top of a piece of paper and pin it on the wall.

My Goal

REMEMBER TOO THAT YOUR GOAL CAN CHANGE.

In our late teens and early twenties we evolve massively and you might find that your priorities **change**. It's useful to keep revisiting your goal and checking whether it's still what you **genuinely** want. Doing this will hugely streamline the process of making life decisions, moving forward.

HOW TO DECIDE WHETHER TO DO MORE OR LESS OF SOMETHING

'For this first type of decision, you should consider how the decision of doing more or less of something will impact your goal,' says Dr Barnard. We're told from a very early age that we can divide certain choices and behaviours into 'good' and 'bad' but, more of a good behaviour and less of a bad one isn't necessarily helpful. For example, exercise is always presented as a 'good' behaviour, but we also know it can be addictive. Unless your goal is to become a professional athlete, spending huge amounts of time exercising is probably going to detract from your overall life goal. So your aim should be to ringfence **time** to exercise, so you can still get the chemical benefit to your wellbeing but it doesn't **take over** your life.

Remember the graph on page 38? There is a **'point of diminishing returns'** on almost everything – how ambitious the targets you should set for yourself should be, how much you should stress or worry about things, or even how confident you should be. The most successful people recognize that, just like a Mary Berry recipe, it's all about getting your quantities right.

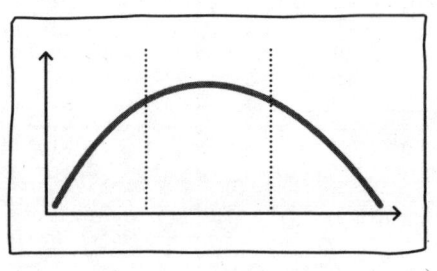

HOW TO DECIDE THE BEST OPTION

Dr Barnard's second method can be used for any decision that involves whether to do something or not to do something, for example, **should I go to university straight away or take a gap year?**

According to Dr Barnard, 'what makes these types of decisions so difficult is that we can never accurately predict what the outcome of our decision would be'. He suggests thinking only about the **best-case and worst-case outcomes** for each path. What will the maximum upside for us be if it really works out? What will be the maximum downside if it doesn't? Draw yourself a chart like this:

	PATH 1	PATH 2
BEST-CASE OUTCOME		
WORST-CASE OUTCOME		

Quantify each outcome out of ten then subtract the downside points from the upside points. The biggest number is probably what you should do (unless your gut is screaming **'NOOOOOOOOOOOOOOOO!'**).

CONFIDENCE BOOSTERS

Wherever the next chapter of your life is taking you, chances are you're going to need some extra reserves of confidence to make that leap. Below are some tools you might find useful:

MINDFULNESS

There are aspects of the road ahead which **you cannot anticipate or plan for**. You must reconcile yourself to this. If, like me, you're always imagining the worst-case scenario (for every potential new experience I concoct some twisted waking nightmare – usually resulting in my untimely and painful death) **mindfulness can really help**. As previously mentioned, mindfulness draws you into the moment, thus silencing (or at least quieting) those inner voices which obsess about the past or worry about the future. One is unchangeable, the other unpredictable so, in reality, fretting about either is a complete waste of energy.

Simple mindfulness techniques like controlling your breathing can help take the edge off any new and potentially scary situation in which you find yourself spiraling into panic.

AFFIRMATIONS

Many people swear by 'affirmations' to help counteract a negative inner monologue and train their brain to think more positively.

Basically, affirmations comprise a pre-planned phrase you say to yourself several times per day, ideally in front of a mirror and representing a belief you would like to hold about yourself. Our unconscious brain learns through **repetition**, so the idea is that after a while the phrases will be absorbed into our unconscious belief systems, at which point they will have 'sunk in' and will counteract any destructive and self-limiting beliefs.

The problem I find with affirmations is they can sound a bit arrogant, particularly if you're British. Show me a British person who can stand in front of a mirror chanting 'I am beautiful and magnificent' with a straight face and I'll show you someone who probably has American parents. I've therefore suggested some British affirmations which are pleasingly non-up-themselves:

- I am good enough
- I deserve just as much as the next person
- I am alright
- Everything is going to be okay
- Ultimately, we're all going to die anyway and no one has their exam results on their headstone

(That last one might have been a joke. Although do use it if it's helpful.)

PRACTICE

I get asked constantly by teenagers what the **'secret to being confident'** is. I wish I could tell them such a thing exists. I know I seem like a person who has my shiznay together, but the truth is there is no magic age at which you suddenly wake up and feel 'confident', or know the meaning of anything. Everyone is just pretending to know what they're doing.

Confidence is really just **practice**. The first time you do anything it is by definition terrifying because it is unknown. The second time it is slightly less scary because you know what to expect . . . and so on and so forth until you can do it without a second thought.

Use any opportunity you can to practise. Take the train or drive the route from home to your new place of work in advance. Visit the town your new uni is based in if you can and have a wander around to get your bearings. Take your washing to a local launderette and practise doing it there if that's what you'll be doing at uni. Give yourself a budget, do a food shop and try to eat only what you have bought for a week. Join a new club for the summer, or go to a gig by yourself so you have practised walking into a room of people you don't know and striking up a conversation with someone.

hello

EXPERIMENT WITH THE FUTURE AS MUCH AS YOU CAN WHILST YOUR CURRENT SAFETY NET IS STILL IN PLACE.

SECTION 6
THE CONTRACT

WHETHER IT'S PARENTS OR CARERS constantly disturbing your homework and revision with 'helpful' motivational tips/enquiries as to your progress, or siblings distracting you by playing music at ear-bleeding volume/trying to kill each other outside your bedroom door, the desire for your parents and you to do well at school is going to test the relationship between you and whoever you live with.

Virtually everyone experiences a veritable rollercoaster of annoyance, irrational hatred, door-slamming and verbal slanging matches when you're feeling the pressure – and particularly when it comes to exam time – and there's a comfort in knowing this. **You stressed + parents stressed = highly charged environment** in which everyone's a bit angry for no real reason. This is to a certain extent unavoidable, but being prepared can help minimize distress for everyone involved.

I asked Philippa Perry, a psychologist who wrote *The Book You Wished Your Parents Read* for her thoughts. She said:

'To most of these parents and guardians you need to remind them that they need to "back off" but you have to do it kindly otherwise they have hurt feelings and you've enough to worry about without having to be guilty as well. So to do this you will have to show them you understand [their perspective].
I suggest saying this:

> 'I know you want the very best for me and your trying to help comes from being very kind, loving, good people, but when you ask me what I'm revising and tell me how important it is, I just feel rage brewing up inside me. I may not do as well as you dream, but if you had a bit more confidence and trust in me that would help me to believe in myself. You are right I may need help and encouragement and reminders to work, but I wonder, nay plead*, if you might help me in a way I suggest rather than what you believe is most helpful. And as well as studying I need to relax to regain my equilibrium, which is why I haven't got a text book in my hand right now. I will be sure to let you know if there is anything you can do.'

You might also wish to put it all into a contract, so everyone is aware of what is expected of them and you have set some healthy parameters. Use the templates overleaf (you can amend it to include anything specific that applies to your family):

---

* You can translate this so it sounds like you. I don't know anyone apart from Philippa who would say 'nay plead' in a real-life situation (most of us can only aspire to her levels of fabulousness).

CONTRACT: FOR PARENTS AND CARERS

Contract between ....
(hereafter referred to as 'The Student') and

....
(hereafter referred to as 'The Parent').

Preliminaries

The Student would like it known that he/she/they are more than aware that all schoolwork and exams are important. They have been told this approximately four thousand times by absolutely everyone. However their demeanour might appear, they are experiencing a level of anxiety about this. Having read *Yes You Can: Ace School Without Losing Your Mind,* The Student understands that their academic performance hinges to a certain extent on minimizing stress.

The Parent would like it known that they are human too and just trying to be helpful.

Term of Contract

This contract is valid during term time and at any point during evenings or weekends when the Student might be engaged in school work.

Covenants

The Student promises to:

- Plan their study and homework timetable as realistically as possible.
- Maintain balance and look after their mental health to the best of their ability using the tips in this book.
- Do their best.
- Not blame The Parent if their best falls short of their own expectations.
- Do something really nice for The Parent at the end of particularly stressful times, such as the examination period (such as cooking them a meal).

The Parent Promises to:

- Trust The Student to plan their schoolwork and to execute this plan in a timely fashion.
- Not 'check in' on the Student every five minutes demanding to know where they are up to with their study.
- Trust The Student when they say they are conducting finite 'stress bucket' emptying activities and not assume they are malingering.
- Demonstrate that they are proud of The Student whatever the outcome of their school report or exams may be.

Signed:

.... The Student

.... The Parent

Date: ....

This contract whilst (unfortunately) **not legally binding**, will encourage you to think about what you need from the people around you during this potentially stressful time.

In my experience, most conflicts can be resolved or avoided if you're able to articulate **what** exactly the other person has done, **why** it isn't helpful and what you'd like them to do **instead**. If you do find yourself having to have one of these types of conversations, try:

> 'When you do ....
>
> It makes me feel ....
>
> Right now I need ....
>
> So I was wondering if you could try ....
> ....'

I've yet to meet anyone who was so cold-hearted that they didn't at least pause momentarily when asked to change their behaviour in this way. They might get defensive and they might not ultimately change, but at least you have been clear.

REMEMBER, THE ONLY PERSON'S BEHAVIOUR YOU CAN ACTUALLY CONTROL IS YOUR OWN.

CONCLUSION

> 'Never let success go to your head; Never let failure get to your heart.'
>
> Anonymous

PEOPLE TEND to look back on their pasts with reality-distorting nostalgia. When we assess past periods of time, our brains cherry-pick the highest and lowest points, figuring that these have the capacity to teach us the most. Our brains catalogue memories in moments, rather like a filing cabinet, so it can pluck out any useful entries when figuring out what it wants to replicate and what it wants to avoid. The mundane or mid-range experiences usually get lost in all the drama.

That might explain why, amidst all the discussion about the rollercoaster of emotions which tend to make up our experience of studying, I haven't mentioned what you'll probably feel most:

BOREDOM.

Make no mistake, a huge bulk of your revision will be really, **tediously** boring. It's the boredom we feel most acutely at the time of exams and then immediately forget, replacing it with memories of squeaky-bummed terror in the exam hall and light-headed euphoria/crushing disappointment on results day.

It requires so much **self-discipline** to tear yourself away from far more diverting and enjoyable activities (e.g. playing video games, socializing, watching paint dry) and force yourself to go back over stuff you have already learned (and, in some instances, didn't find that interesting to begin with). For all our talk of stress, panic and anxiety, when you're actually going through the exam period, it's probably the relentless boredom which is the hardest to cope with.

I hope this book, with its tips on study techniques that match your motivation and how to incorporate as many senses as possible into the studying and revision process will help combat the mundanity somewhat.

REMEMBER: ANY SUBJECT HAS THE POTENTIAL TO BE INTERESTING IF YOU CAN MAKE IT RELEVANT TO OR RESEMBLE WHAT YOU ALREADY ENJOY. (EVEN ALGEBRA.)

I also hope you've learned some **life hacks** to help you face the thornier aspects of school. For many people, their teenage years are the first time they have had to deal with extreme pressure. That's why people in their twenties and beyond still wake up bathed in sweat the night before a job interview or other scary event, having dreamt they're back in a room with their school bully, have an 800 word essay due the next morning or are re-sitting their senior school exams.

Our brains defer to the first experience we had of something which made us fearful in the way that major life events do. The important thing to bear in mind is that, as well as being a stepping stone to the next chapter of your life, exams are a rite of passage which can teach you a lot about who you are – and that's true of both the **positive** and the **negative** aspects.

People who have only ever had positive life experiences fall broadly into two categories:

- **Super-privileged people who have been anaesthetized by their circumstances from any of the consequences of their failures**
- **Super-gifted people who breeze through experiences that others find challenging**

Both of these types of people generally turn out to be asshats.

TRULY HAPPY AND SUCCESSFUL PEOPLE HAVE EXPERIENCED BOTH HIGHS AND LOWS AND DON'T DEFINE THEMSELVES BY EITHER.

THEY SEE FAILURE AS A LESSON TO BE LEARNED AND SUCCESS AS A LESSON WHICH HAS BEEN APPLIED. THEY KNOW THAT BOTH GOOD AND BAD DAYS ARE TRANSITORY. WHATEVER THIS PHASE OF YOUR LIFE LOOKS LIKE, YOU CAN EMERGE FROM IT ENHANCED.

By completing the activities in this book, you now know **what is happening** in your brain when you get stressed or anxious.

You know which activities **keep you sane** and the importance of incorporating them into a busy schedule. You know whether you're a lark, a night owl or neither. This is vital knowledge that will help you win at this ridiculous game we call 'life'.

Whilst you might never need to know what differentiates a cumulonimbus cloud or the angles of an isosceles triangle ever again, many of the lessons – academic and personal – that you learn in your school years and using this book to guide you through these times of huge change will give you some valuable transferrable skills for the future.

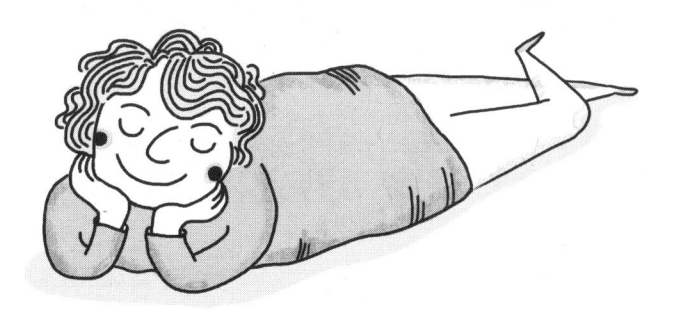

MOST OF ALL, THOUGH, I HOPE I'VE CONVINCED YOU THAT ACING SCHOOL DOESN'T HAVE TO MEAN LOSING YOUR MIND.

GOOD LUCK . . .

FURTHER INFORMATION, ADVICE & SUPPORT

If reading this book has made you realize that you or a friend need further support or information on mental health, please, I beg of you, **DO NOT GOOGLE IT**. The internet is a fantastic resource, but it's also sprinkled liberally with misinformation, dangerous pro-self-harm, eating disorder and suicide groups posing as support forums and people selling snake oil.

To help you access safe, genuinely informative and evidence-based support on a variety of issues related to mental health, I recommend the organizations below:

THE MIX www.themix.org.uk 0808 808 4994
Whatever your preferred method of communication, you'll find it at The Mix. They have an online discussion board, helpline, text service as well as articles written by young people on everything from sex, to money to mental health. They also have experts drop in to conduct Facebook chats and webinars.

YOUNG MINDS www.youngminds.org.uk
Parent Helpline: 0808 802 5544
Young Minds are a kick-ass organization campaigning for change in order to make sure young people experiencing mental health difficulties get the support they need. Their website is packed with useful information and they also have a dedicated helpline for parents who want to know how to support children with mental health issues.

BEAT   www.beateatingdisorders.org.uk   0808 801 0677

Beat is the UK's leading eating disorder charity. You'll find information on all aspects of eating disorders and recovery, such as what you can expect if you go to your GP seeking help. There are also accounts written by young people with first-hand experience of eating disorders and a directory of services on their website.

THE NATIONAL SELF HARM NETWORK   www.nshn.co.uk

The National Self Harm Network is an online support forum which is available 24/7. It is also closely monitored, which means users can discuss self-harm and related issues safely, without fear of triggering.

CALM   www.thecalmzone.net   0800 58 58 58

The 'Campaign Against Living Miserably' is an anti-suicide charity that particularly focuses on providing mental health support for men. They have some incredible awareness campaigns and videos which are moving, informative and highly shareable.

NO PANIC   www.nopanic.org.uk   Youth Helpline: 0330 606 1174

No Panic is a charity specializing in self-help techniques which support recovery from anxiety disorders. You'll find information on the skills you need to manage panic and anxiety on their website and you can also become a member to receive regular updates.

HEAD MEDS   www.headmeds.org.uk

If you have been advised to take medication for your mental health and want more information, you can type the brand name into Head Meds' search engine and find information on what the medicine actually is and does, any side-effects, what to expect when taking it and written accounts from people who have done so.

STUDENT MINDS www.studentminds.org.uk
Student Minds is a student mental health charity. They work in sixth forms and universities to provide support programmes for students experiencing mental health issues, as well as campaigning for better provision.

THE COUNSELLING DIRECTORY www.counselling-directory.org.uk
If you're looking for a private therapist, just type your location into Counselling Directory's search engine. This generates a list of counsellors in your area, giving you access to their qualifications, areas of expertise and contact information.

THE HUB OF HOPE www.hubofhope.co.uk
Also downloadable as an app, the Hub of Hope allows you to see a list of all mental health support providers near you and how far away they are (it's basically the Tinder of mental illness). You can also filter your search according to the specific issue for which you're seeking help.

EXPERTS
If you want to read more about the experts who contributed to this book, here's where you can find their work:

SECTION 1: UNDERSTANDING YOUR BRAIN

Dr David Bainbridge
David is a science writer, reproductive biologist and veterinary anatomist at the University of Cambridge. One of his specialist areas is adolescence and his book *Teenagers* was published in 2009. Find out more at **www.pdn.cam.ac.uk/directory/david-bainbridge**

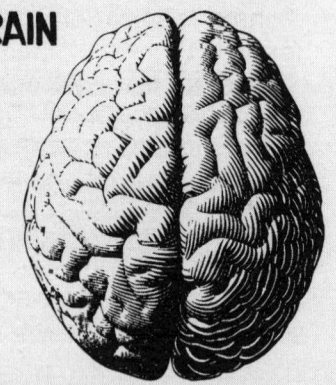

Dr Thomas Curran
Tom worked at the Centre for Motivational and Health Behaviour Change at University of Bath until 2019, where he did some ground-breaking research on perfectionism and it's psychological impact. He now works at the LSE. You can listen to his TED Talk at www.ted.com/talks/thomas_curran_our_dangerous_obsession_with_perfectionism_is_getting_worse?language=en

SECTION 3: PREPARATION AND TIME MANAGEMENT

Rachel Riley
Rachel is a TV presenter and mathematician. She currently co-presents the Channel 4 daytime show *Countdown* and its comedy spin-off *8 out of 10 Cats Does Countdown*. Follow her on Twitter/Instagram at **@RachelRileyRR**

Pasha Kovalev
Pasha is a professional dancer, specializing in ballroom and Latin American styles. He is best known in the UK for his seven-year stint on *Strictly Come Dancing* and he has also appeared on *So You Think You Can Dance?* and *Dancing With the Stars*. Follow him on Twitter **@PashaKovalev**

SECTION 4: TESTS AND EXAMS

Shahroo Izadi
Shahroo is an expert in addiction and behavioural change. She has worked in NHS substance misuse services and now has her own practice, as well as being a consultant for the Amy Winehouse Foundation. Her book *The Kindness Method* was published in 2018. Find out more at **www.shahrooizadi.co.uk**.

Claire Eastham
Claire is an award-winning blogger and specialist on anxiety. Her book *We're All Mad Here: The No-Nonsense Guide to Living with Social Anxiety* was published in 2016. Find out more at **www.allmadhere.co.uk**.

SECTION 5: THE NEXT CHAPTER

Dr Alan Barnard
For more than 20 years, Alan has researched how to create practical decision support methods and apps which can help people overcome limiting beliefs. Find out more at **www.dralanbarnard.com**.

Cathy Walker
Cathy is Head of Education at the Girls Day School Trust (GDST). For more info go to www.gdst.net. Thanks to Sarah White, Deputy Head at Sheffield Girls, Darren Payne, Deputy Head at Shrewsbury High School and Rebecca Halse, Deputy Head at Nottingham High School for contributing to the 'year 8 to 9' section.

SECTION 6: CONTRACTS

Philippa Perry
Philippa is a psychotherapist and author. She has presented several documentaries about mental health and is currently *Red Magazine's* agony aunt. Her book *The Book You Wish Your Parents Had Read (And Your Children Will Be Glad That You Did)* was published in 2019. Follow her on Twitter **@Philippa_Perry**

ABOUT THE AUTHOR

Natasha Devon MBE has been touring schools, colleges and universities throughout the world for more than a decade, delivering talks and conducting research on mental health and related issues. She is a trustee for the charity Student Minds and a patron for No Panic, an organization helping people manage anxiety. She has founded several campaigns including the Mental Health Media Charter and Where's Your Head At?, which aims to improve mental health in work places. She lives in West London with her husband Marcus and her cat, China Girl.